GREAT
TED
TALKS
LEADERSHIP

Portable Press
An imprint of Printers Row Publishing Group
10350 Barnes Canyon Road, Suite 100, San Diego, CA 92121
www.portablepress.com • mail@portablepress.com

Portable Press
Publisher: Peter Norton • Associate Publisher: Ana Parker
Senior Developmental Editor: April Graham Farr
Senior Product Manager: Kathryn C. Dalby

Produced by Quarto Publishing plc
Publisher: Mark Searle
Creative Director: James Evans
Art Director: Katherine Radcliffe
Commissioning Editor: Sorrel Wood
Managing Editors: Isheeta Mustafi and Jacqui Sayers
In-house Editor: Abbie Sharman
Editor: David Price-Goodfellow • Designer: Tony Seddon

Library of Congress Control Number: 2019949968
ISBN: 978-164517-217-8

Printed in China

24 23 22 21 20   1 2 3 4 5

GREAT
TED
TALKS
LEADERSHIP

An Unofficial Guide with
Words of Wisdom from
100 TED Speakers

HARRIET MINTER

**PORTABLE
PRESS**

San Diego, California

CONTENTS

INTRODUCTION

What do we mean by leadership? It would be easy to confine leadership to the workplace or to say it's something we do when we want to influence others, but as these 100 TED talks show, leadership can show up anywhere and everywhere. And some of the toughest directing we will have to do in our lives isn't over others but ourselves.

Great leaders bring together a mix of skills and values to decide a pathway into the future. In this book, I've highlighted the key traits I've seen in great leaders time and time again, from resilience to authenticity, via bravery and empathy. That is not to say that these traits are fundamental to leadership—I'm sure we all know people in positions of power who show none of them. However, I hope that by bringing them together in this book we'll start to shape the kind of leadership we want to see in the future.

TED is based on the principle of one simple idea being able to change the world. In this book, there are 100 ideas that I hope will bring about some sort of change for you as a leader. You don't have to read it from start to finish in numerical order (although if that makes the most sense to you, please do so), but I would suggest you try to find a little nugget of wisdom from each of the chapters. That way, you'll gain a rounded sense of what it means to be a leader in today's world. If a particular piece of advice really resonates with you, you may want to watch the whole talk, and so we explain on the opposite page how to watch the talks online for free.

Not all of the talks are about leadership directly—in fact, I'd say the majority aren't. I believe that it is this broader knowledge that gives us the tools to adapt and grow as leaders. It also gives us somewhere to turn to when we are in need of inspiration. So, if you come across a talk that feels a little abstract, take extra time to listen to it and see what thoughts it sparks. The lessons I have learned from these TED talks will not be the final ones they have to share.

How to Use This Book

This book of tips is designed to be quick and easy to skim through. You can read it from front to back or back to front, or dip in and out whenever you need inspiration—it's completely up to you. And if you want to refer back to a tip later but can't remember where it is, that's no problem. At the back of the book are two indexes—one for topics, and one for the speakers quoted—so it's always easy to find what you're looking for.

Crucially, you don't need to have seen a single TED talk to enjoy this book. But maybe you'd like to deepen your learning and watch one of the talks now? Again, that's no problem, as at the time of publication, all of the talks are available to watch free online.

You will find the links to the talks included in this book as part of the speaker index. Or you can simply go to ted.com, click on the magnifying glass in the right-hand corner, and type in the title of the talk. For example, to find the first talk mentioned in the book (on page 10), you'd type "How I Held My Breath for 17 Minutes."

Occasionally, though, a talk might not be there. During the production of this book, a few of them hadn't yet made it onto the TED website. But don't worry: they're all available to view on YouTube too. In other words, if a talk doesn't come up when you type it into TED.com, go to YouTube.com and search there instead. In this case, be sure to put the title in quote marks (" ") so that YouTube knows exactly what it's looking for (there are a few billion other videos on the site, so it pays to be specific).

Alternatively, you might prefer to type the title into Google (again, surrounded by quote marks). In that case, the talk should appear in Google's listings under the "Videos" heading.

Whether you choose simply to read the book or use it as a stepping-stone to the wider universe of watching TED talks, it's time to open your mind and be inspired. Prepare to get a whole new perspective on your life and profession and where it can take you!

BE RESILIENT
no matter what's happening around you

Leadership isn't a one-day job—you have to turn up again and again in the face of adversity. This chapter teaches you how to stay motivated even when it feels like nothing is going your way.

PREPARATION IS KEY

Build in time to practice—nobody beats a world record the first time out the gate.

How long can you hold your breath underwater? David Blaine holds the world record at just over seventeen minutes, but when he set out to achieve that goal he was way off target. In his, literally breathtaking, talk the performer describes what motivated him to go for the world record and what he learned along the way.

All of Blaine's work requires intense preparation—for this particular event he spent fifty-five minutes each morning practicing breath-holding techniques. This made him tired and ill, but he kept going because he knew the importance of preparation. His first attempt failed, but he came back and tried again.

Blaine knew that if his second attempt was going to succeed he had to keep his heart rate down. For the first five minutes, it looked like he was going to fail as his heart rate climbed up and up. Then he started to feel pains across his body, his limbs went numb, and he felt a desperate urge to breathe. Nevertheless, he stayed underwater—and long enough to beat the world record and prove that the impossible is indeed possible.

> ## "MAGIC, WHETHER I'M HOLDING MY BREATH OR SHUFFLING A DECK OF CARDS, IS PRETTY SIMPLE. IT'S PRACTICE, IT'S TRAINING AND EXPERIMENTING, WHILE PUSHING THROUGH THE PAIN."
>
> **DAVID BLAINE**

🔍 FIND OUT MORE

David Blaine's talk:
"How I Held My Breath for
17 Minutes"
2009

When we look at a big goal, it's very common to assume that because no one else has achieved it, we won't either. However, with the right preparation we can build ourselves up to a point where suddenly what seemed like a giant leap becomes a small step. We can push ourselves further and harder than we believe possible, but to do that we must practice, fail, practice more, and try again. And we can't give up—not even when it feels like we're drowning. Also see Ashton Cofer's talk on page 86 or Paula Hammond's talk on page 185.

HOW FAILURE CULTIVATES RESILIENCE

By putting ourselves in situations where there is a chance we might fail, we build up our resilience to stress.

What if failure wasn't something to be feared, but something that was necessary to build resilience? Raphael Rose works with NASA—an organization whose motto is "Failure is not an option"—to look at the effect failure has on us and how we can recover from it.

Far from seeing failure as something to be avoided, Rose believes it is one of the greatest teachers we can have and the key to a more fulfilled life. Resilient individuals put themselves in situations where they might fail but where they also might grow—in other words, they go outside their comfort zone. In his talk "From Strength to Resilience," Rose uses the example of a student who signed up for an advanced math class, asked out a prom date, and joined the debate team. All those situations had the possibility of success or failure, but by simply taking part in them the student built up her resilience levels. Even if she failed, she would have learned something from the experience, and surviving failure would build her confidence.

To build our resilience, we have to put ourselves in situations that might seem foreign or challenge our set behaviors. Rose recommends starting small, being compassionate to ourselves, and engaging in something meaningful. Doing something for the joy it brings, and accepting that sometimes we might fail, lowers our stress levels and builds our resilience.

FIND OUT MORE

Raphael Rose's talk:
"From Strength to Resilience"
2018

BELIEVE IN YOURSELF

Sometimes the voices in our head will tell us to quit,
but we can choose to ignore them.

Polio survivor Minda Dentler was tired of handing out water on the sideline while her family competed in sports. At the age of twenty-eight she was introduced to handcycling, and six years later she decided to take on the legendary Kona Ironman World Championship in Hawaii.

Halfway through the bike portion of the event, Dentler realized she's never going to be able to finish the race within the time limit and had to quit. If you've ever had to give up halfway through something important, then you'll relate to the feelings of devastation Dentler was experiencing. It was only when she talked to a colleague about her failure that she gained any perspective on the situation. The colleague said to her, "Big dreams and goals can only be achieved when you're ready to fail."

As leaders, we often face tasks that seem insurmountable. Dentler suggests breaking the big tasks up into smaller, more manageable segments, but accepting that even when we do so we might still face failure. It's at this point that our internal voice will start telling us to quit, and that it's not worth sticking with something when we might fail. But if we can push that voice to one side and just focus on the finish line, we might find ourselves going farther, and faster, than we ever believed we could—just as Dentler did when she completed the Ironman event on her second attempt.

Q FIND OUT MORE

Minda Dentler's talk:
"What I Learned When I Conquered the World's Toughest Triathlon"
2017

Also try Luma Mufleh's talk:
"Don't Feel Sorry for Refugees—Believe in Them"
2017

ENJOY THE JOURNEY

When we focus only on the goal, we miss out on the beauty of where we are now.

Polar explorer Ben Saunders isn't floored by much, but he was somewhat flummoxed when presented with the following questions: "Philosophically, does the constant supply of information steal our ability to imagine or replace our dreams of achieving? After all, if it is being done somewhere by someone, and we can participate virtually, then why bother leaving the house?"

What puzzled Saunders particularly was that when he looked at his own experiences it did seem as though he had spent a lot of his life doing things that were rather unpleasant. At twenty-six, he had traveled to the North Pole and dealt with conditions that were described as the worst since records began. However, he believes that there is something addictive about getting out of the house and doing things: "It seems to me, therefore, that the doing—you know, to try to experience, to engage, to endeavor, rather than to watch and to wonder—that's where the real meat of life is to be found, the juice that we can suck out of our hours and days."

So often we focus on leading our teams toward a specific goal and remain so focused on hitting this that we don't appreciate the journey. What Saunders suggests is that the journey itself is actually the place where we find joy and excitement. As leaders, we can give ourselves energy and excitement for a tough task by focusing on enjoying the journey, and we can encourage our teams to do the same.

Q FIND OUT MORE

Ben Saunders's talk:
"Why Bother Leaving the House?"
2012

THE QUESTION ISN'T WHETHER OR NOT YOU'RE GOING TO MEET ADVERSITY, BUT HOW YOU'RE GOING TO MEET IT.

AIMEE MULLINS

06/100

SHARE YOUR PROBLEMS

We all have a right to be seen and heard. Sharing our problems with those around us can help us get through them.

Emtithal Mahmoud wrote her first poem about the genocide taking place in Darfur, Sudan. She felt as though the tragedies that were happening there were invisible, but when she started reading her poems to her classmates, they asked why she was talking about such depressing subjects. "In that classroom, when all the students started taking their seats and I began to speak—despite this renewed feeling that I didn't deserve to be there, that I didn't belong there or have a right to break the silence. As I talked, and my classmates listened, the fear ebbed away. My mind became calm, and I felt safe. It was the sound of our grieving."

We can shy away from conflict and the fear that if we open up the difficult conversations we're inviting more problems into our world. But as leaders, when we give people time to talk and to express what they're feeling, we actually give them space to heal. And this is the same for us. Leadership doesn't mean having all the answers or carrying all the problems on your own shoulders. Sharing what's going on for you, how you're feeling, and your life experiences allows you to heal those experiences and leaves you ready to move on. Learn how sharing a problem helped rescue 33 Chilean miners in Amy Edmondson's talk on page 120.

Q FIND OUT MORE

Emtithal Mahmoud's talk:
"A Young Poet Tells the Story of Darfur"
2016

Also try Jane McGonigal's talk:
"The Game That Can Give You Ten Extra Years of Life"
2012

IN THE PLACES WHERE I LEARNED TO CRY THE MOST, I ALSO LEARNED HOW TO SMILE AFTER.
EMTITHAL MAHMOUD

EAU CLAIRE DISTRICT LIBRARY

YOU CAN'T KNOW EVERYTHING

As a leader, you'll face problems for which there seems no answer. Instead, focus on what you can do.

There are roughly half a million hazardous objects floating in orbit around Earth, yet currently we track only around 1 percent of them, explains astrodynamicist Moriba Jah. Some are as small as a speck of paint, but when traveling at the right speed even these tiny fragments could cause untold damage to our infrastructure.

It would therefore seem like a good idea to have some sort of map that tracks all these objects, but as Jah explains, not only do we not have the technology to do that, but the information changes depending on who you talk to. The result is that we have a galaxy filled with very crowded space highways and no way of controlling the flow of traffic.

This is often how it feels in leadership—you can see that there is a problem, but you have neither the data nor the resources to solve it. When faced with this situation, it's worth remembering the approach Jah took—map what you can, collect as much data as you can, and keep talking to everyone about it. The key is not to be overwhelmed by what you don't know, and instead focus on what you do know and go from there.

Q FIND OUT MORE

Moriba Jah's talk:
"The World's First Crowdsourced Space Traffic Monitoring System" 2019

Also try Niki Okuk's talk:
"When Workers Own Companies, the Economy Is More Resilient" 2016

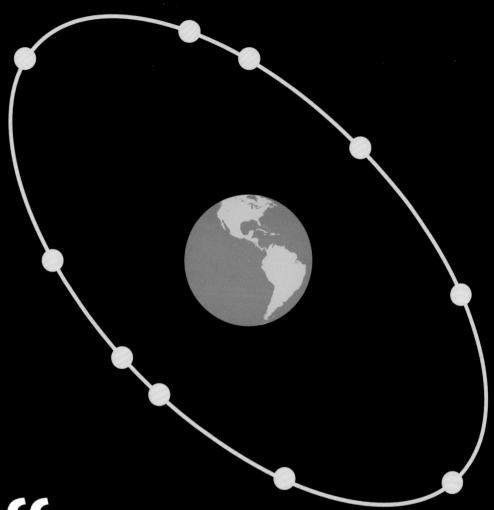

> ## ASK FIVE DIFFERENT PEOPLE WHAT'S GOING ON IN ORBIT . . . AND YOU'RE PROBABLY GOING TO GET TEN DIFFERENT ANSWERS.
> **MORIBA JAH**

FIND YOUR COMMUNITY

A key component of resilience is community. Find those fighting the same fight as you are and allow them to lift you up.

A love story that shows the power of art and community is the focus of Aja Monet and Phillip Agnew's talk, but it also shows us why it's so important to have people to pull us out of the tough times, to encourage and support us, and to show us what's possible.

As Monet says, "While winning awards, accolades and grants soothed so many egos, people were still dying and I was seeking community. Meeting Agnew brought so much joy, love, truth into my life, and it pulled me out of isolation. He showed me that community and relationships wasn't just about building great movements. It was integral in creating powerful, meaningful art, and neither could be done in solitude."

When leaders feel like they're trying to create change in a landscape that simply doesn't want to change or will not accept it, they can isolate themselves. When we do this we can find ourselves drowning in depression, but when we surround ourselves with community we can find other people who are trying to bring about change and who are engaged in making things happen.

We'll talk about the power of collaboration later in the book but for now be reminded that a key part of resilience is finding your community. This will keep you going when it feels, as Monet says, "like we have to scream."

Q FIND OUT MORE

Aja Monet and Phillip Agnew's talk: "A Love Story About the Power of Art as Organizing" 2018

DATA RARELY MOVES PEOPLE BUT GREAT ART ALWAYS DOES.
PHILLIP AGNEW

LEAN IN TO PAIN

Without pushing through difficult times, we simply won't grow.

Austin Eubanks survived the 1999 Columbine High School shooting. It left him with the question, "How do we define pain?" Is it just about the physical responses we feel, or is there an emotional element too? And why are we so keen to avoid it?

After the shooting, Eubanks was prescribed pain medication to treat the physical symptoms he was suffering, but he soon realized that they were much better at numbing his emotional pain. In fact, they were so good that when he tried to stop taking them he couldn't, and he became a drug addict.

What this made Eubanks realize is that we're too quick to try to smother emotional pain rather than actually dealing with it. He describes how he finally made a recovery when he learned to lean into the pain rather than trying to avoid it. Often, we can try to find a way around the difficult or painful problems, but when we go through the pain we experience growth. As Eubanks puts it, "By finding a way to endure through significant suffering, you can actually have meaningful development of personal character." Our society pushes us to find quick fixes for tough issues, but true leadership means accepting that sometimes you have to go through dark times to get to the light at the end of the tunnel.

🔍 FIND OUT MORE

Austin Eubanks's talk: "What Surviving the Columbine Shooting Taught Me about Pain" 2017

> **ACHIEVING POST-TRAUMATIC GROWTH REQUIRES THAT YOU LEAN INTO THE PAIN. YOU CAN'T MEDICATE IT AND YOU CAN'T AVOID IT.**
> **AUSTIN EUBANKS**

HOPE CONQUERS ALL

When you're exhausted and feel like you can't go on, you need to develop an attitude of radical optimism.

> ## IT IS FAR MORE RADICAL AND DANGEROUS TO HAVE HOPE THAN TO LIVE HEMMED IN BY FEAR.
> **SULEIKA JAOUAD**

You might have heard of the hero's journey—a mythical look at how we overcome difficulties in our lives. For cancer survivor Suleika Jaouad, however, myths weren't good enough. She needed an actual journey to help her move on from cancer.

Jaouad explains how being in the midst of a cancer crisis was easier for her to deal with than the aftermath. She was focused on surviving and beating cancer, but once it was gone she felt lost. For many of us, being in a crisis situation gives us a goal to work toward and our adrenaline kicks in, but when the crisis has passed, we're left exhausted and unsure of what to do next. As Jaouad puts it, "being cured is not where the work of healing ends. It's where it begins."

When we've been through a difficult or stressful situation, we may want to cling to safety and avoid being hopeful in case those hopes are dashed. On a 15,000-mile road trip, Jaouad learned the power of optimism. As leaders, we will often experience setbacks or failure, but to be able to lift our heads up, pull ourselves together, and try again, we have to have

optimism—we have to believe that the best could happen even if the odds are against us. When we have that, we start to feel enthusiasm for the world around us again and we're ready for the next challenge. This "radical, dangerous hope," as Jaouad describes it, is what propels us on to the next challenge and gives us the energy to keep fighting.

Q FIND OUT MORE

Suleika Jaouad's talk:
"What Almost Dying Taught Me About Living"
2019

STRESS IS YOUR FRIEND

Science has traditionally considered stress to be a bad thing, but by learning to see it as a performance enhancer, our health can actually benefit from it.

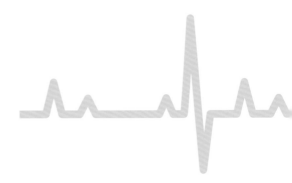

Do you see stress as bad for your health? That's how Kelly McGonigal saw it until she found a study that showed people who had experienced extreme stress, but who saw it as helpful rather than harmful, had the lowest rate of stress-related death.

It turns out that stress itself isn't bad for our health; it's believing that stress is bad for our health. What McGonigal discovered was that when we reframe our thinking so that our stress responses—such as a pounding heart or faster breathing—are seen as helpful for our performance, our body behaves in a much healthier way. "It actually looks a lot like what happens in moments of joy and courage. Over a lifetime of stressful experiences, this one biological change could be the difference between a stress-induced heart attack at age fifty and living well into your nineties. And this is really what the new science of stress reveals—that how you think about stress matters."

As you move up the leadership ladder, you'll be faced with bigger and more stressful situations. If so, you want to manage your physical health at this time and then start seeing stress as a good thing. And the other thing you can do, McGonigal suggests, is to lead others to embrace it too. Those of us who go out and care for others are less affected by the negative aspects of stress—in fact, we actually recover from stress more quickly. See also the talks on pages 33 and 183.

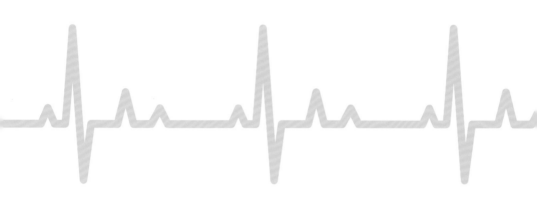

"

WHEN YOU CHOOSE TO VIEW YOUR STRESS RESPONSE AS HELPFUL, YOU CREATE THE BIOLOGY OF COURAGE. AND WHEN YOU CHOOSE TO CONNECT WITH OTHERS UNDER STRESS, YOU CAN CREATE RESILIENCE. "

KELLY MCGONIGAL

🔍 **FIND OUT MORE**

Kelly McGonigal's talk:
"How to Make Stress Your Friend"
2013

BE EMPATHETIC
to others but also to yourself

Empathy is the new buzzword in leadership. Gone are the days of command and control, and instead we want leaders who can bring an emotional connection to their teams. This chapter explains why empathy is a skill that can be taught and how to do it.

TALENT, NOT CIRCUMSTANCES

It's easy to make assumptions about people based on their circumstances, but when we do this, we often miss out on their true talent.

Can you look at people's talents rather than their circumstances? As leaders, we like to think that we value our team members based on their talents rather than their personal situation, but so often that's not the case. Our unconscious biases mean that we tend to judge people without even realizing we've done it, and then we put them in pigeonholes and miss the talents they might be hiding.

Working with homeless and disabled artists, social entrepreneur Liz Powers found that people would often see only their social circumstances and not their talents. When she met Scott, a homeless man who'd been creating art for more than thirty years, she found an incredible talent. Thanks to her company, Scott's artwork now hangs in the offices of politicians and sells for tens of thousands of dollars. Powers saw his talent regardless of his circumstances.

Powers has a mantra of highlighting the positive rather than the negative. Instead of focusing on the fact that someone is homeless or disabled, she looks instead at the skills they have and makes sure she pulls these talents out of them. She's noticed that when she does this, the individual in question has more energy for the other areas of their life. As leaders, we can choose to see the negative or the positive in those we work with, but if we want an energized and uplifted team, we should—like Powers—focus on the positive.

Q FIND OUT MORE

Liz Powers's talk:
"A New Way to Define Self-worth"
2016

"

WHAT OTHER TALENTS ARE OUT THERE, ESPECIALLY FOR INDIVIDUALS WHO HAVE CHRONIC UNEMPLOYMENT? HOW CAN WE HELP THEM GET THEIR TALENTS OUT THERE AND CONTRIBUTE TO THE ECONOMY? "

LIZ POWERS

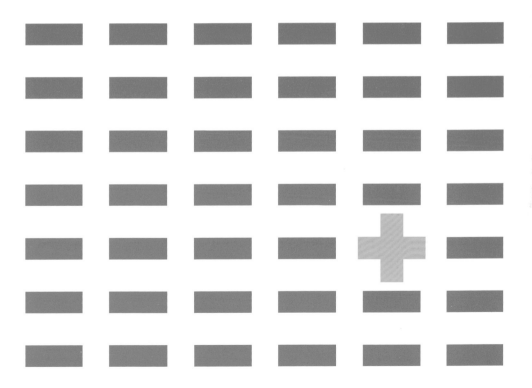

HAVE DIFFICULT CONVERSATIONS

We tend to ignore or argue with people who disagree with us, but when we stop and just listen to them, we can often find common ground.

Have you ever left a snarky remark on somebody's YouTube video or Instagram post? If so, then you might one day find yourself on the phone to Dylan Marron.

Marron creates online content. He's used to being challenged and trolled, but one day it got to be too much and he decided to sit down with his detractors and ask them the simple question "Why did you write that?" What he learned surprised him. When he confronted them, most of the people who had been abusing him online seemed nice enough. They'd had problems in their lives that they told Marron about—they'd been bullied in school or were also being trolled online. He found himself empathizing with them, but this empathy confused him. How could he feel empathy for people who fundamentally disagreed with him and everything he stood for? How could he like a man who wrote homophobic slurs under his videos?

What Marron came to learn is that it's possible to feel empathy and kindness toward someone even when you don't agree with them. As he puts it, "empathy is not endorsement." What he means by saying this is that it's safe to sit down and to listen to people that you disagree with, and that doing so doesn't make you weak and it doesn't mean your views are simply being sidelined. Displaying empathy to someone who we might find challenging gives both parties the chance to see the other side of the argument and this can start to build bridges.

🔍 FIND OUT MORE

Dylan Marron's talk:
"Empathy Is Not Endorsement"
2018

Also try Sam Richards's talk:
"A Radical Experiment in Empathy"
2010

PRIORITIZE MENTAL HEALTH

We're all used to looking after our physical health, but we need to be just as vigilant when it comes to our mental health.

"Why is it our physical health is so much more important to us than our psychological health?" asks psychologist Guy Winch. We wouldn't tell somebody with a broken leg just to walk it off, but when people tell us they're suffering with mental health difficulties we tend to shrug it off and hope they'll sort it out themselves.

To be great leaders, we have to be ready to look after both our own mental health and that of our team members and colleagues. Winch calls this "emotional first aid." Within this, he explains that when we are suffering from a mental health issue—particularly something like loneliness or isolation—we can begin to think that others care less about us than they actually do.

If, as leaders, we want our team members to know that we care about them, then we have to reach out to them actively and make sure they know we want to hear what is going on with them. When we practice emotional first aid with others, it has the added benefit of being good for our own minds. In reminding others to be compassionate to themselves, we remind ourselves of the same thing. And by encouraging others to reach out, we become part of their community and increase our own. This emotional first aid builds our empathy muscle and supports those around us.

Q FIND OUT MORE

Guy Winch's talk:
"Why We All Need to Practice Emotional First Aid"
2014

CHECK YOUR PRIVILEGE

When we understand where we sit on the social pyramid, we empathize better with other people and can begin to understand how they see us.

It might seem strange to say that we can learn about empathy through advanced mathematics, but that's what Eugenia Cheng's talk encourages us to do.

If you hated math at school, don't worry—Cheng takes a complicated formula and uses it to explain simply why some of us are more privileged than others and how this privilege then impacts our behavior toward each other. She uses her formula to unravel the layers of privilege that come with gender and race, slowly working through it to explain why it's good to be a woman but better to be a white woman. Or good to be black but better to be a black man than a black woman.

As Cheng points out, it's when we start to look at the layers that go into our individual identity that we start to see why our experience of the world is unique, and also why other people's experience of the world has influenced them in the way it

has. So often, a discussion around privilege sinks into a "well, my life is harder than yours because . . ." battle, but what Cheng shows us is that by using a formula to analyze human experience, we can easily see the areas where each of us wins or loses.

Cheng talks about her own experience as a woman of color and how that has both helped and hindered her, and she also looks at the way in which she is better off than others. Her entire talk is a beautiful display of empathy at its most simple and powerful. And it also gives us a very easy way to understand team dynamics and how our own leadership can affect the feelings of those around us.

🔍 FIND OUT MORE

Eugenia Cheng's talk:
"How Abstract Mathematics Can Help Us Understand the World"
2018

"
WE ARE ALL MORE PRIVILEGED THAN SOMEBODY AND LESS PRIVILEGED THAN SOMEBODY ELSE. "
EUGENIA CHENG

16/100
SEEK ALTERNATIVE VIEWS

Even if you love an idea, deliberately seeking out people with alternative viewpoints on it can help you see the bigger picture and catch possible issues early on.

Have you ever been so in love with an idea that you've completely failed to see the flaws in it? Even when other people have tried to show you how the idea might fail, you've ignored them and blundered on. When an idea succeeds, we call this blindness "faith," but sometimes our faith leads us to ignore everyone else's views and experiences.

Director Adong Judith believes that the idea of "staying in your truth" has become a fixation for some. As she points out, by staying in our truth we're instantly assuming that someone else's truth must be wrong. We've taught ourselves that when we believe in something we have to push it as hard as we can, but as Judith points out, by doing this we miss the chance for critical conversations. We need to get people with different viewpoints around the table with us—it's the only way our ideas can be challenged and adjusted.

So, the next time you have an idea you feel strongly about, ask yourself, "Who might disagree with me here? Who might have a different way of looking at this that I haven't thought of yet?" Then gather those people together and ask for their opinions. Share your opinions, too, and listen to everybody. When you do this, you start to see the bigger picture, not just your own viewpoint.

For more advice on how to manage difficult conversations check out Daniel Goleman's talk on the importance of asking questions (page 44) or Isaac Lidsky's talk on unconscious bias (page 159).

Q FIND OUT MORE

Adong Judith's talk:
"How I Use Art to Bridge Misunderstanding"
2017

Also try Dalia Mogahed's talk:
"What It's Like to Be Muslim in America"
2016

"

I BELIEVE NO ONE IS IGNORANT. WE ARE ALL EXPERTS, ONLY IN DIFFERENT FIELDS. "

ADONG JUDITH

EMPATHY SAVES LIVES

True leadership is not just telling people what to do; it's also holding the space for them to find the path for themselves.

One of the bravest things we can do as leaders is to allow people to bare their souls to us in full without prejudging them. As Eldra Jackson shares how he came to spend nearly a quarter of a century in jail in his talk, you can see the bravery it takes him to tell a story he's clearly not proud of.

Jackson's early life experiences taught him that respect and power were the most important things, and that they must be gained at all costs. "A sense of power equaled strength in my environment and, more importantly, in my mind," he says. However, when he was moved to a new prison he was invited to join a group that other prisoners called "hug-a-thug." This was a talking therapy group that aimed to challenge the structural way of thinking most of the male prisoners had grown up

with. Without participating in a group that listened to him without judgment but with the empathy to challenge him in a kind manner, Jackson would have continued his life as a criminal.

When we create space for people to be honest about who they are and when we listen to their stories, we give them the opportunity to challenge their self-beliefs and to grow from this. Challenging and empathizing with those around you requires leadership, and while this is a tough ask, it's one with great rewards.

🔍 FIND OUT MORE

Eldra Jackson's talk:
"How I Unlearned Dangerous Lessons About Masculinity"
2018

· ·

Also try Michele L. Sullivan's talk: "Asking for Help Is a Strength, Not a Weakness"
2016

> **THE GREATEST WAY TO MASK A SHAKY SENSE OF SELF IS TO HIDE BEHIND A FALSE AIR OF RESPECT.**
> **ELDRA JACKSON**

ADD RATHER THAN SUBTRACT

While it can be exciting to rip up the rule book, sometimes it's better to work with the world around us.

When we think about augmented reality, we often think of artificial intelligence creating worlds that we can't even imagine. But the true purpose of technology, argues Galit Ariel, should be to add on to the world that is already around us.

Ariel explains that augmented reality is the ability to amplify what is already there rather than ripping it all up and starting again. As leaders, we often want to be seen as the people creating new worlds, coming up with the big vision and taking our followers into a completely new universe. However, a better approach can be to see what we can add to what is already there. Asking people to step into the complete unknown can be scary or confusing for them, but when we take something they already understand and enhance it with our own ideas and values, it is much more easy to accept. We need to use technology to connect ourselves to reality—a new reality, yes, but still reality. When we leave reality behind completely, we create fear, loneliness, and isolation.

So when you're developing a new idea, check it for sense with the people around you. How do they relate to it? How far out of their comfort zone is it pushing them? Can you find a way of linking this new idea to the world around you? It might challenge our technological boundaries, but how can it add to what is already there rather than wiping that out altogether?

Q FIND OUT MORE

Galit Ariel's talk:
"How AR Can Make Us All Feel More Connected to the World"
2018

EMPATHY IS A PRACTICE

How do we know what other people are feeling? We pay close attention to them and look for the universal language of emotion.

There is a universal language that we nearly all understand: the language of emotional response. In his talk "You Are Fluent in This Language and Don't Even Know It," artist Christoph Niemann explores some of the images that we all understand, regardless of our cultural backgrounds—such as the Wi-Fi symbol showing a strong Wi-Fi connection, which promotes a feeling of relief and happiness within us. Or two people struggling for control of the armrest on a crowded airplane. Or the eternal problem of wanting to spoon your partner but not knowing what to do with the arm that gets trapped underneath.

When we use images to show an emotion, we can communicate with people beyond language. But to do this, we have to tune into the feelings of those around us, and that requires us to pay more attention. Niemann spent Sundays studying a random object and seeing what emotions or references it linked to in him.

Imagine what would be possible if we all paid that much attention to the people around us? By really tuning in to the people we lead, how they respond and react to the situations we create, we can start to develop worlds that inspire all of us. This is the practice of empathy, and like all practices, the more we do it the better we become at it.

Q FIND OUT MORE

Christoph Niemann's talk: "You Are Fluent in This Language and Don't Even Know It" 2018

YOUR INTERACTION WITH AN IMAGE, YOUR ABILITY TO READ, QUESTION, BE BOTHERED OR BORED OR INSPIRED BY AN IMAGE IS AS IMPORTANT AS MY ARTISTIC CONTRIBUTION.

CHRISTOPH NIEMANN

RESPECT IS KEY

When faced with someone who fundamentally disagrees with you, how do you persuade them? Empathy and respect.

> ## WE OWE IT TO ONE ANOTHER AND OUR COUNTRY TO REACH OUT AND TRY TO CONNECT. WE CAN'T AFFORD TO HATE THEM ANY LONGER.
> **ROBB WILLER**

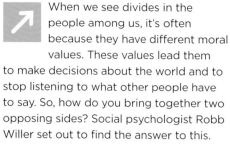 When we see divides in the people among us, it's often because they have different moral values. These values lead them to make decisions about the world and to stop listening to what other people have to say. So, how do you bring together two opposing sides? Social psychologist Robb Willer set out to find the answer to this.

What Willer found was that when two opposing sides argued for their point of view, they did so based on the moral values they believed to be most important, not the moral values of their opponent. Essentially, they were trying to convince their own side.

How do you persuade someone who disagrees with you of the value of your argument? Willer explains, "If you want to persuade someone on some policy, it's helpful to connect that policy to their underlying moral values. And when you say it like that, it seems really obvious. Right? Like, why did we come here tonight? It's incredibly intuitive. And even though it is, it's something we really struggle to do. You know, it turns out that when we go to persuade somebody on a political issue, we talk like we're speaking into a mirror. We don't persuade so much as we rehearse our own reasons for why we believe some sort of political position."

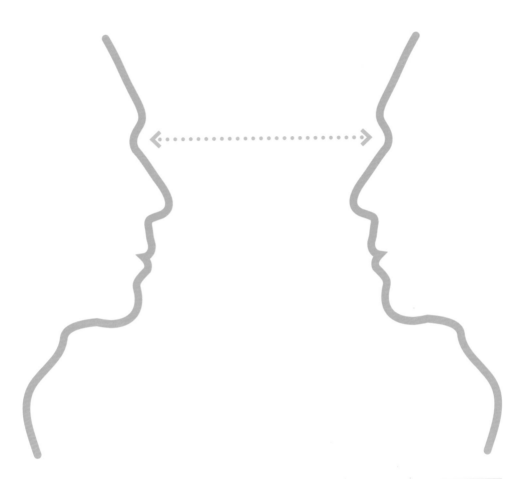

But how do we rehearse the argument for the other side instead of putting across our own view? Willer believes the answer is simply "empathy and respect." If you want to bring people over your side, take the time to understand where they're coming from and respect their right to have their own opinion.

🔍 **FIND OUT MORE**

Robb Willer's talk:
"How to Have Better Political Conversations"
2016

ASK QUESTIONS

How long does it take you to ask someone else about themselves? Talk less, listen more, and see the difference it makes to your leadership (and your dating).

Why, when we all have so many opportunities to help others, do we do it only some of the time?

We all have the ability to be compassionate to others and yet we exercise this compassion only in certain circumstances. Why is that?

Psychologist Daniel Goleman set out to discover what makes us help some people and not others. He found that while our default wiring is to help others most of the time, our attention is often elsewhere and we miss the other person's needs. We are so focused on our own thoughts, needs, and emotions that we forget to ask other people about theirs.

Goleman points out that this happens particularly during dating. He recalls that one woman rated her potential dates based on how long it took them to ask her a question with the word "you" in it. Try it yourself the next time you have a conversation with someone. How much time do you spend talking about yourself, and how much time do you listen to what is going on with the other person?

This tuning in to other people is a skill, and like all skills it requires constant practice and refinement. In fact, our ability to do this—to empathize with other people—is what separates us from psychopaths. As leaders, we should aim to talk less and listen more. Can you honestly say you do that?

Q FIND OUT MORE

Daniel Goleman's talk: "Why Aren't We More Compassionate?" 2007

COMMUNICATE WITHOUT WORDS

Sometimes people can't tell us they need help; we have to look for the signs.

When Laurel Braitman adopted her dog, she didn't expect him to come with a full-blown anxiety disorder. Unlike dealing with a human suffering from a mental illness, Braitman couldn't simply ask her dog what was going on with him, so she had to learn to interpret the signs.

Braitman relates this to people: "Just because you ask someone that you're with . . . how they feel doesn't mean that they can tell you. They may not have words to explain what it is that they're feeling, and they may not know. It's actually a pretty recent phenomenon that we feel that we have to talk to someone to understand their emotional distress. Before the early twentieth century, physicians often diagnosed emotional distress in their patients just by observation."

When we know someone well, we can pick up on the signs if something isn't right with them, and we need to learn to trust our instincts on this. If we notice that someone we spend a lot of time with is behaving differently, it is on us to step up and ask them about it. This can feel uncomfortable and awkward, but a key component of leadership is the ability to sit in that discomfort for the sake of someone else. When we lead a group of people, we should spend enough time getting to know them that we can notice when their behavior changes. That way, we can adapt to try to help them.

🔍 FIND OUT MORE

Laurel Braitman's talk: "Depressed Dogs, Cats with OCD—What Animal Madness Means for Us Humans" 2014

UNDERSTAND YOUR CUSTOMER

If men won't go to a health clinic but they will go to a barbershop, then why not put the health clinic at the barber's?

Joseph Ravenall grew up going to the barbershop with his father. While it might have looked like a shop where you got your hair cut, Ravenall saw it as much more than that. He saw it as a place where men could share stories and learn from each other. In particular, he saw it as a place where men could talk about their health, sharing stories of how to look after themselves better in a way they wouldn't do at home.

When he became a doctor, Ravenall saw the barbershop as a way to engage men in their health. He started working on healthcare solutions that would appeal to African American men and found that if health clinics offered a barber service then more men would come along. Even better, he discovered that barbers were happy to carry out health checks—they would learn how to test blood pressure and offer this as a service when men came in for a haircut.

Ravenall took the time to understand how his patients ticked, what made them feel comfortable, and how to reach them, and in doing so he's saving their lives. To truly help people, we must first understand their behaviors and adapt our products to them, rather than expecting them to adapt to the product.

Q FIND OUT MORE

Joseph Ravenall's talk: "How Barbershops Can Keep Men Healthy" 2016

> WHAT IS YOUR BARBERSHOP? WHERE IS THAT PLACE FOR YOU WHERE PEOPLE AFFECTED BY A UNIQUE PROBLEM CAN FIND A UNIQUE SOLUTION?

JOSEPH RAVENALL

BE VISIONARY and bring others with you to create that vision

When we think of great leaders, we often think of inspiring visionaries such as Steve Jobs or Martin Luther King Jr. This chapter looks at what it means to have a vision and how you can convince other people to back you.

THE POWER OF LANGUAGE

How do the words we use and the emotions they convey help us to bring people into our vision?

How do you convey your vision to other people? Javed Akhtar would like us to spend far more time thinking about the words we use and the impact they have on people.

In this talk on the power of language, Akhtar argues that words are the things that unite us, allow us to pass on our experiences and cultures, and ultimately separate us from animals. When we have a vision we're excited about, we can get so carried away with it that we forget to be picky about the language we use around it. We forget the power of words to affect how people feel and so we don't use them to their true advantage.

Akhtar argues that we need to spend more time on choosing our words, and he's correct. Really thinking about the words we use adds depth and weight to our ideas. When you're choosing the words you're going to use to convey your vision, think about the language your audience has grown up with. What words reflect their culture and their history? How can you tap into their experiences and emotions through language? If you can do this, you'll find it easier to bring them on the journey with you and truly convey why your vision is so important. Being a true leader means being able to slow down and use your words to carry people along with you.

Q FIND OUT MORE

Javed Akhtar's talk:
"The Gift of Words"
2017

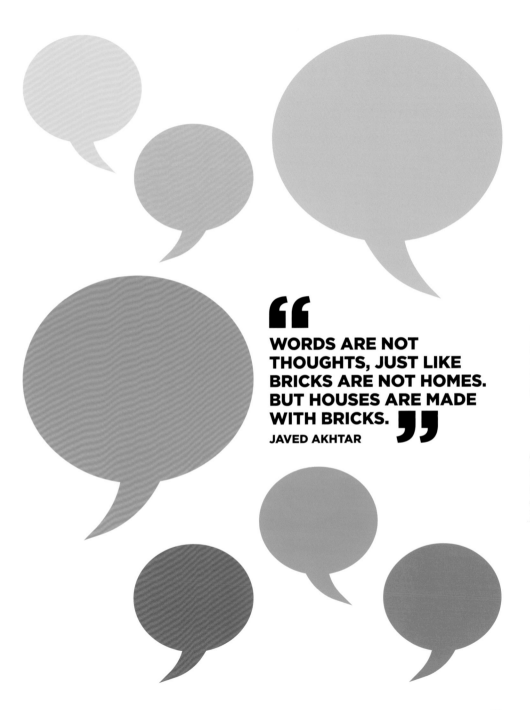

WORDS ARE NOT THOUGHTS, JUST LIKE BRICKS ARE NOT HOMES. BUT HOUSES ARE MADE WITH BRICKS.

JAVED AKHTAR

HIDDEN VISIONARIES

You don't have to have an MBA to be a visionary—anyone, anywhere can have a dream and turn it into a reality.

In her role as a journalist, Gayle Tzemach Lemmon set out to meet entrepreneurs who didn't match the typical example. She explains, "I went to Afghanistan in 2005 to work on a *Financial Times* piece, and there I met Kamila, a young woman who told me she had just turned down a job with the international community that would have paid her nearly $2,000 a month—an astronomical sum in that context. And she had turned it down, she said, because she was going to start her next business, an entrepreneurship consultancy that would teach business skills to men and women all around Afghanistan."

Kamila's resilience, determination, and vision inspired Lemmon. She realized she had assumed Kamila's story would be limited by her circumstances, but in fact these difficulties had made Kamila's dream even bigger. This happened again and again with the largely female entrepreneurs Lemmon met.

The world has a set idea of what a successful visionary looks like—generally a white man from a wealthy country. But just because you don't meet these criteria doesn't mean you have to dream small. Often, being different from the norm means that our visions cater to a market that has been ignored up to now. If you believe in your vision, it doesn't matter who you are or where you come from—you have the opportunity to bring other people with you and to change all your lives.

Q FIND OUT MORE

Gayle Tzemach Lemmon's talk: "Women Entrepreneurs, Example Not Exception"
2011

GET THEM ON BOARD

You can have the greatest vision in the world, but if you can't bring people with you, it will never be anything more than an idea.

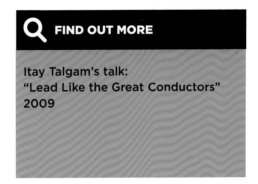

Conductors are charged with turning noise into music, and when they stand in front of an orchestra they can feel as though they are completely responsible for that transformation. But of course that's not the case. In front of them is a group of people who must all work together to realize that vision of bringing a piece of music to life.

In his talk on the role of a conductor, Itay Talgam explains why having a vision is important and why nothing will come from it if you don't bring people with you. He tells the story of a great conductor, who everyone loved but who the orchestra didn't want to work with. The conductor was so keen to control his vision for the music that there was no room for the orchestra members to develop or grow— they felt like they weren't allowed to add to his vision and so they grew bored with it.

When leaders feel strongly about their vision, they still need to hold it lightly; they need to bring in the skills and talents of their orchestra to take the vision from idea to reality. Allow people to see your vision but also to add to it, to build on it and be a part of it. That way you will go from simply having a vision to leading the team that creates it.

Still having problems getting people on board with your idea? Check out how you can work with them rather than against them with Galit Ariel's talk on adding to ideas (page 39).

Q FIND OUT MORE

Itay Talgam's talk:
"Lead Like the Great Conductors"
2009

27/100
MAKE IT FUNNY

When we use comedy to convey our vision, we connect people to it on a deeper level.

Stand-up comedian Kasha Patel isn't just a comedian, she's also a science writer who works for NASA. She realized early on that she could use jokes to help explain complicated science and bring people with her on journeys that might feel far removed from their daily lives.

To try to work out what makes a joke relatable, Patel analyzed 500 of her jokes. When she did so, she realized her science jokes made up just 25 percent of her repertoire but performed 40 percent better than her other jokes. Why was this? Patel had found that her audience were often overwhelmed by science—it felt too foreign or complicated for them. But when she broke science down into facts and myths, she could make people laugh and explain concepts to them. To make a joke work, she first had to define what she wanted that joke to do—what was it she wanted people to learn from it? Then she tried to work out how she could make the joke as truthful, and relatable, as possible. What she learned from this is that people want to hear the truth. They want to be able to trust in the vision, but to do this they need to be able to see how it impacts on their life and it needs to be entertaining.

If you're not sure you're someone who is naturally funny, then Patel's formula looks like this: write out your premise or vision and then work out all the different punchlines—in other words, what turns the premise on its head or would be a surprising outcome? Pick the ones that best fit your audience and watch as you bring your vision to life for them.

FIND OUT MORE

Kasha Patel's talk:
"The Benefits of Using Comedy to Explain Science"
2018

Also try Chris Bliss's talk:
"Comedy Is Translation"
2011

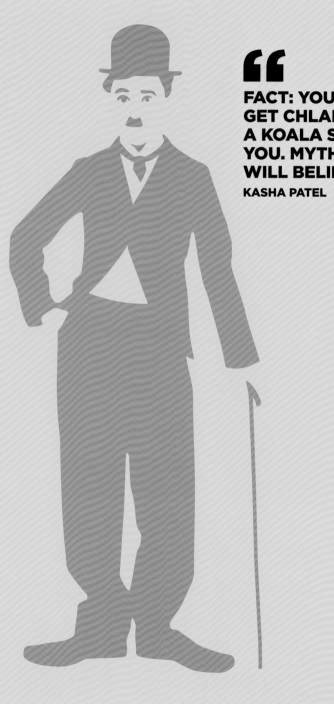

"

**FACT: YOU CAN
GET CHLAMYDIA IF
A KOALA SCRATCHES
YOU. MYTH: YOUR WIFE
WILL BELIEVE YOU. "**

KASHA PATEL

SOLVE A PROBLEM

If you don't know where to find your vision, look at the problems you want to solve.

Majd Mashharawi's home is in Gaza, Palestine. For the past ten years she has been living in darkness for much of the time due to the lack of electricity and working infrastructure. Rather than either accepting the situation or being trodden down by it, Mashharawi asked the question, "What can I do for the people around me; how can I help them?" She didn't wake up one morning with a vision, but instead looked at the world around her and asked how she could make it better.

If you could change one thing about the world around you, what would it be? How could you make life better for people? What would you do if you had to solve the problem? Asking these questions is how you start to find your vision.

Mashharawi's vision was to create something useful out of the ruins and rubble that surrounded her. It took her 150 attempts, but she finally created a building block from rubble and ashes, and her community can now use these blocks to repair destroyed houses and to build new ones. Mashharawi's vision wasn't to create a new building material; it was to bring safety and security to the people around her. The building block she created was the tool that allowed her to achieve her vision.

FIND OUT MORE

**Majd Mashharawi's talk:
"How I'm Making Bricks Out of Ashes and Rubble in Gaza"
2018**

. . . .

**Also try Kiran Bedi's talk:
"A Police Chief With a Difference"
2010**

IN GAZA, WE HAVE A WHOLE LOT OF NOTHING. AND I AIM TO CREATE SOMETHING FROM THAT NOTHING.

MAJD MASHHARAWI

KNOW THE WHY

Vision isn't based on what or how, but on why. It's this "why" that brings people into our vision.

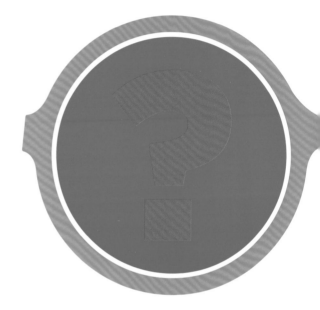

In one of the most watched TED talks of all time, Simon Sinek explains the importance of knowing why we do the things we do. Having studied organizations and leaders for decades, Sinek concludes that there's one thing that sets visionary leaders and companies apart from their competition: they know why they do the things they do. In other words, they have a purpose, and they are driven by that purpose.

This "why" is not an external thing but an intrinsically held internal belief or cause.

It's something that resides deep inside and cannot be ignored—the calling, as Sinek puts it, to "get out of bed in the morning." One of the things that makes Sinek's talk so groundbreaking is that he challenges the typical business notion of trying to appeal to as many people as possible.

For Sinek, visionary leadership isn't about bringing everyone with you, but about bringing the people who also believe what you believe with you. When we appeal to people's values and belief systems, we talk to the part of their brain that controls decision-making rather than

> **PEOPLE DON'T BUY WHAT YOU DO; THEY BUY WHY YOU DO IT.**
> **SIMON SINEK**

the part that analyzes and worries. This part of the brain doesn't care about logic; it cares about feelings and emotions. And when we stimulate it, we can bring people into our vision with us.

If you need some help finding your "why" check out Olympia Della Flora's inspiring talk on how she turned around the most difficult children in her school (page 70) or find a mentor who can help guide as did Tai Lopez (page 78).

FIND OUT MORE

Simon Sinek's talk:
"How Great Leaders Inspire Action"
2009

Also try Simon Sinek's talk:
"Why Good Leaders Make You Feel Safe"
2014

USE YOUR IMAGINATION

Don't wait to be told it's possible—dream big.
Then make the dream possible.

When movie director James Cameron first pitched the idea for *Avatar*, he was told it was impossible. He wanted to push the boundaries of computer-generated images and make a film that depicted realistic humans in an animated world. Even though the technology for this didn't exist, Cameron believed it was possible. However, the resistance he faced was such that he found himself putting the project to one side.

Cameron then went on to direct *Titanic* and, as he puts it, used the film as an excuse to get the production company to fund an exploration of the actual shipwreck. Again, everyone told him it wouldn't be possible—that he wouldn't be able to get down there or that the film company would never want to pay for it. Yet Cameron believed it was possible, and he made it happen.

Our hopes and dreams don't just have to stay out there in the ether—they can become the visions we use to propel our reality. If Cameron hadn't been a keen scuba diver who was determined to find a way to make it down to see the *Titanic* wreck, the film probably would never have been made. He used his passion to create a vision, and then he kept pushing until he found a way to make this vision a reality.

What we learn from Cameron's talk "Before *Avatar* . . . a Curious Boy" is the power of having a really clear vision and the tenacity to believe you can make it come true. A few years later, the director revived his *Avatar* idea and the film was made—and with it, what was possible in moviemaking shifted completely. Remember, just because your vision seems impossible doesn't mean that it is.

Q FIND OUT MORE

James Cameron's talk:
"Before *Avatar* . . . a Curious Boy"
2010

"

IMAGINATION IS A FORCE THAT CAN ACTUALLY MANIFEST A REALITY. "

JAMES CAMERON

KNOW YOUR IMPACT

If you think your vision is to sell a lot of something, you're thinking too small.

When Harish Manwani started working at Unilever, his boss asked him why he was there. Harish replied, "To sell a lot of soap." His boss's response? "No. You're here to change lives."

Manwani had been looking at the detail of what he did and had failed to see the bigger picture. Yes, he was going to sell a lot of soap, but that soap was going to stop the spread of infection and stop people dying from diseases.

It's very easy for all of us to get caught up in the day-to-day details of what we do. We look at spreadsheets and bottom lines, and we think about five-year plans and deliverables. But every so often we need to take a step back and ask ourselves, "What is the impact of our work?" And when we're trying to find the vision for our company, we can ask, "What would we like the impact of our work to be?"

As a leader, your job isn't to get caught up in everyday issues, but to hold the vision of a bigger impact. Leaders know why their team members are doing what they're doing, and they also know and communicate the importance of making that vision bigger than a bar of soap.

Q FIND OUT MORE

Harish Manwani's talk:
"Profit's Not Always the Point"
2013

**IT'S NOT ABOUT
SELLING SOAP, IT'S
ABOUT MAKING SURE
THAT IN THE PROCESS
OF DOING SO YOU CAN
CHANGE PEOPLE'S LIVES.
SMALL ACTIONS, BIG
DIFFERENCE.**
HARISH MANWANI

VISION REQUIRES SACRIFICE

If you really believe in your vision, you will sacrifice everything to make it work—even yourself.

Could you walk away from your dream if you realized you were the thing standing in the way of it becoming a reality? This is what Julius Maada Bio did when he gave up being head of state for Sierra Leone.

In 1992, Bio was part of a military coup whose leaders promised to return democracy to the country and put power back in the hands of the people. This didn't quite come to pass, but when Bio found himself head of state four years later, he set out to ensure there would be democratic elections—even if it meant he wouldn't be elected.

Bio had a vision for Sierra Leone, and this vision was bigger than his own needs and desires. When we realize this as leaders, we pass on a different energy to our team. We show them that success is really not about promoting ourselves or increasing our own power, but bringing the vision to fruition. We show our team the belief we have in that vision, and in doing that we make it even more powerful.

Leaders also allow that vision to spread out beyond themselves. When Bio walked away as leader of his country, he did so in the knowledge that he had made space for others to follow in his footsteps. This was part of Bio's vision, and also a way of ensuring it remained. His legacy was far greater than his time in office and his vision still lives on, through other people and also through him when he was democratically elected as president.

FIND OUT MORE

Julius Maada Bio's talk:
"A Vision for the Future of Sierra Leone"
2019

USE YOUR HISTORY

Who we are and where we come from can shape the vision we hold for ourselves and the world around us.

Ory Okolloh grew up in Kenya. She left to go to Harvard and become a lawyer, but she found herself returning to her home country as an activist. Okolloh was tired of hearing people complain about how the entire continent of Africa was depicted around the world and she wanted to actively change that.

In her talk "How I Became an Activist," Okolloh explains that it's very easy for us to sit on the sidelines of a problem or to even remove ourselves from it completely. We might literally move cities, countries, or continents, or we might just pretend that there's nothing we can do about it and so we carp from the sidelines instead.

True leadership is knowing that even if the answer isn't instantly accessible, we still show up and fight for what we believe to be right and true. For Okolloh, this meant giving up a well-paid job in the United States and returning to Kenya. She talks about her father's death and her own anger at how her family had been treated badly when she was a child owing to their poverty. It is here, in these injustices, that Okolloh finds her vision.

It wasn't duty that took Okolloh back to Africa, but a passion to change things and bring about a more equal society across the globe. However, to find this passion she had to confront painful issues in her past and decide how she would respond to them in the present. What is there in your past that could fuel your vision?

 FIND OUT MORE

Ory Okolloh's talk:
"How I Became an Activist"
2007

VISION NEEDS REALISM

If we're to create a vision that truly changes things, then first we need to be honest about the situation.

When Aubrey de Grey began researching age and aging in our society, he found that some people just didn't want to think about the problem. While de Grey was wondering how we could help people live longer, healthier lives, a whole host of people were telling him that aging was inevitable and that he should stop trying to fight it.

When de Grey set out on his vision to find a way to improve the aging process, he thought people would want to be involved with it. But as he says in his talk "A Roadmap to End Aging," it's very easy for people to get wedded to the status quo. If we want to shift them beyond that, we have to be prepared to give them a reality check as well as a vision.

As a leader, you will never get people to support your vision if they can't see that the problem it solves really is that bad. You have to set out your argument, explain why the issue is terrible and needs to be changed, and then fight against the belief that change isn't possible. Often when people tell you that a situation just is the way it is and that nothing can be done about it, it's because they're scared of what it might take to change that situation. To inspire action, your vision not only needs to sell the dream but also needs to present the brutal, honest truth of the reality.

Q FIND OUT MORE

Aubrey de Grey's talk: "A Roadmap to End Aging" 2005

> **AS WITH ANY RADICAL DEPARTURE FROM PREVIOUS THINKING WITHIN A PARTICULAR FIELD, YOU KNOW, YOU EXPECT PEOPLE IN THE MAINSTREAM TO BE A BIT RESISTANT AND NOT REALLY TO TAKE IT SERIOUSLY.**

AUBREY DE GREY

BE STRATEGIC
and bring others with you

A vision is great, but nothing happens without strategy. This chapter teaches you how to develop a strategy, explains why it's important, and suggests how you can deploy it against any problem.

SMALL CHANGES ADD UP

You might think you need a huge budget and an army of thousands to deploy your vision, but you don't.

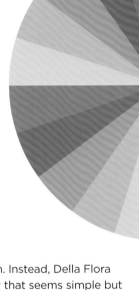

> **" AND HERE'S THE MAGICAL THING: IT DIDN'T COST US A WHOLE LOT OF EXTRA MONEY. WE SIMPLY THOUGHT DIFFERENTLY ABOUT WHAT WE HAD. "**
> **OLYMPIA DELLA FLORA**

For Olympia Della Flora, being a school principal was all about trying to find a way to do more with less. Budgets were tight and the students all seemed to need individual attention and help. In particular, one student, D, regularly caused disturbances. He would throw furniture around the classrooms, yell at teachers, and run out of lessons. Della Flora's time was being eaten up with thinking about how she could change D's behavior.

D was causing such a big problem in the school that it seemed only a big solution would help him—either far more support or exclusion. Instead, Della Flora instituted a strategy that seems simple but had a huge impact. She created a calm space in which D could start the day, she joked or sang with him when she saw him around school, and she brought him in to help with the younger students.

While these were only small actions, regularly executed they had a big impact. When we're thinking about the strategy we need to execute our vision, it's easy to go for the biggest and most elaborate answer. Instead, look at what you already have in your arsenal. What could you adapt to help you put your plan into action?

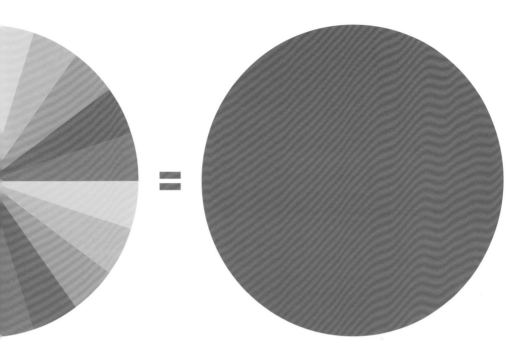

One other thing Della Flora did was to look at the budget she did have and see how it could be used in a smarter way. She understood that putting a bit of money toward emotional support would reap huge academic benefits.

What changes could you make to your current budgets to maximize them? What small steps could your team members take to help them spread the word about what you're doing? Strategy doesn't have to be big to be clever—sometimes it's the little things that count.

 **FIND OUT MORE**

Olympia Della Flora's talk: "Creative Ways to Get Kids to Thrive in School" 2019

STRATEGY BREEDS STRUCTURE

The type of strategy you design will influence not only the steps you take, but also the impact you have.

How do you get your team to execute your vision? Traditional working practice states that the only way to get people to do anything is to give them something at the end of it—we pay people to do a job, offering them an IOU in return for a favor. We believe that people carry out actions for others only when there's something in it for them.

Well, Barry Schwartz argues, that might not be true. He explains that if we do work only if there's money at the end of it, it's because we've created a system where human nature has been taught to see money as the reward for work. The system we have put in place has influenced our own human nature. What this means for you as a leader is that when you're designing the strategy that will execute your vision, you need to think carefully about the impact it will have on human nature.

If your strategy, for example, is to reward anyone who supports your vision with a promotion, the people who are most supportive are those who most want a promotion. If part of your strategy is to take small steps forward and then analyze the results, you might create a system where people become more cautious about their daily tasks. Every action we take has an impact, so we need to think carefully about how our strategy plays into the culture we want to create.

For more ways to break the system, check out Linda Hill's talk on managing creativity (page 128) or Joi Ito's talk on the power of pull (page 178).

FIND OUT MORE

Barry Schwartz's talk:
"The Way We Think About Work is Broken"
2014

Also try Thelma Golden's talk:
"How Art Gives Shape to Cultural Change"
2009

STRATEGY BEATS VISION

It's one thing to have a big vision, but without a strategy behind it, nothing will come to fruition.

Joseph Roche signed up to be one of ten people who would embark on a one-way trip to colonize Mars. He has spent his entire life dreaming of being able to view the stars up close, and his vision is to live his life doing the thing that has fascinated him since childhood—traveling in space.

But what Roche hadn't thought about was what it would take to get him there. In this talk "A Life on Mars," he discusses the strategy he will have to put into place in order to complete his mission to Mars. He will spend ten years in training, learning survival skills and creating a plan with his crewmates for how to make Mars habitable. He will then have to spend seven months in a tiny shuttle, traveling through space, washing with wet wipes and exercising for three hours every day just to make sure his body doesn't decay.

Once on the planet, he'll live in a bubble, unable to step outside for fear of radiation poisoning.

It's very easy to get caught up in the glamour of a vision—let's move to Mars! But without the strategy, nothing is possible. Strategy is the backbone of any vision; it's admitting that at some point something will go wrong and you'll have to plan for it. Strategy makes vision possible—without it, you're just floating in space.

Q FIND OUT MORE

Joseph Roche's talk:
"A Life on Mars"
2014

STRATEGY SHOULD BE HARD

Creating a strategy requires time and effort—you should be able to feel your brain working as you do it.

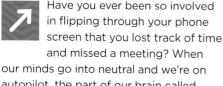 Have you ever been so involved in flipping through your phone screen that you lost track of time and missed a meeting? When our minds go into neutral and we're on autopilot, the part of our brain called "executive function" has stopped working. This function is the thing that helps us figure out problems—it's what keeps us in the present moment, aware of our actions.

Executive function is also responsible for finding strategies to help us get through our daily lives. It's our executive function that, in the example given by Sabine Doebel in her talk "How Your Brain's Executive Function Works—and How to Use It," tells us that if we have to wait to have a second marshmallow, a way of controlling our impulse to eat it is to sit on our hands. In short, executive function helps us build strategies.

What we learn from this is that when we are shaping a strategy we need to be fully present. It's not something we can do while multitasking or mindlessly scrolling through Facebook. Developing a strategy requires us to be focused and actively engaging our brains. Doebel likens this to when you're learning to drive and you have to think through each maneuver before you make it—it should feel like hard work. So, if it feels like the strategy comes easily, go back and look at what you might have missed.

🔍 FIND OUT MORE

Sabine Doebel's talk:
"How Your Brain's Executive Function Works—and How to Use It"
2018

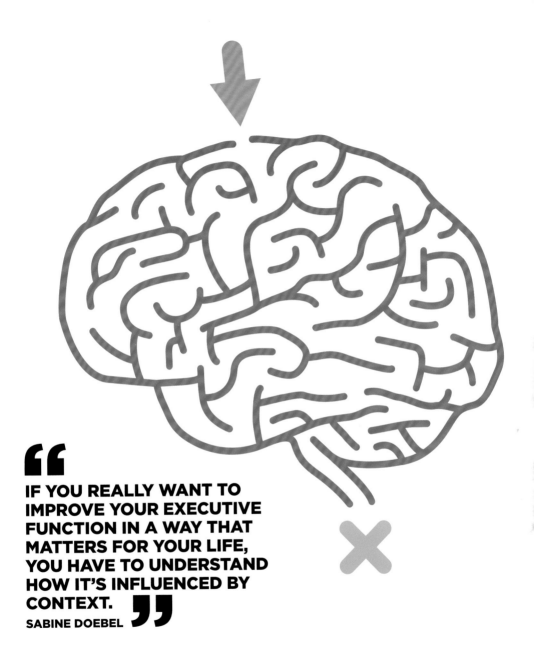

IF YOU REALLY WANT TO IMPROVE YOUR EXECUTIVE FUNCTION IN A WAY THAT MATTERS FOR YOUR LIFE, YOU HAVE TO UNDERSTAND HOW IT'S INFLUENCED BY CONTEXT.

SABINE DOEBEL

KEEP IT SIMPLE

Creating a strategy can feel overwhelming,
so break it down and organize it.

Whether we know it or not, we are all managers. As Anne Johnson points out in her talk "Strategic Planning in Practice," we are all the managers of our own life, even though we are also our only team member. And when we're managing others, we need a strategy to take an idea from a thought to reality.

Too often we get scared off creating a strategy because we feel overwhelmed by what's involved. We're picturing spreadsheets, graphs, and intense analysis of the details. But as Johnson explains, creating a strategy is really very simple. You just need to ask yourself, "What do I need?" This isn't just what you need in terms of actual resources, but also support and structure. What support do you need from your family? What mechanisms can you put in place to keep you focused on your goal?

Once you have established what you need, you can then start to organize yourself and your resources. Break your vision into short-term goals and match each piece of your strategy with these smaller targets. What sits where? What is the order in which things need to happen? Now that you have a fully organized strategy, you can start to execute it.

Q FIND OUT MORE

Anne Johnson's talk:
"Strategic Planning in Practice"
2017

" INNOVATE, STRATEGIZE, ORGANIZE, AND ENERGIZE. IF YOU CAN DO THOSE FOUR THINGS, I BELIEVE THAT WHATEVER STAGE OF MANAGEMENT YOU'RE IN, YOU'RE GOING TO BE SUCCESSFUL. "

ANNE JOHNSON

FIND A MENTOR

You don't have to have all the answers. Finding someone who has already achieved what you want will help you start to see what needs to be done.

> ## THERE'S THIS MYTH THAT YOU HAVE TO GO INWARD TO FIND TRUTH. BUT THE TRUTH . . . IS THAT YOU HAVE TO GO OUTWARD.
> **TAI LOPEZ**

 We don't have to have all the answers ourselves. In this talk on the power of mentors and learning, Tai Lopez explains how his grandfather set him on the path to self-discovery by sending him a package of books. Rather than just tell Lopez what he knew, his grandfather was encouraging him to seek answers from a range of people. He was showing Lopez that there are thousands of people out there who have already done the thinking for you—you just need to go out and discover them.

Sometimes we think we have to find all the solutions on our own, but Lopez believes our ability to copy what someone else has done before us is the greatest predictor of our success in life. We need to seek out the people who have gone before us and ask them to share their wisdom with us, to become our mentor. We can then use their knowledge to help us build a strategy to success.

When you're looking for a mentor, Lopez says, you should look for someone who is ten times ahead of you. That way, they will have made most of the mistakes and had the successes you want to experience—they will be able to guide you and help you build a successful strategy.

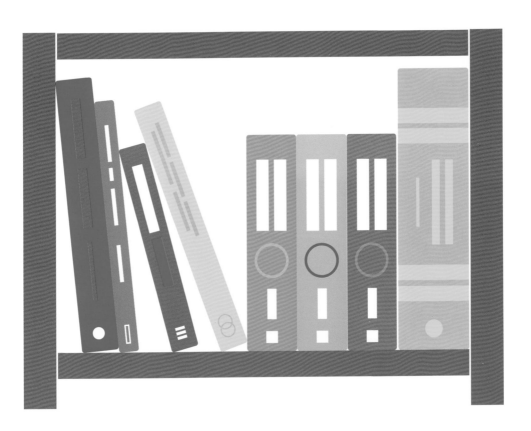

If you bring in a mentor who is only a little bit ahead of you, they're not going to have the experience or wisdom to be able to see all the potential problems you might face. Rather than being able to advise you, they'll be going through these problems with you. So, find a mentor who can help you build your strategy through their own life experience.

🔍 FIND OUT MORE

Tai Lopez's talk:
"Why I Read a Book a Day (and Why You Should Too): The Law of the 33%"
2015

Also try Carla Harris's talk:
"How to Find the Person Who Can Help You Get Ahead at Work"
2018

DON'T FORGET TO FORGET

Use your strategy as an opportunity to let go of things as well as to remember them.

 Raghava KK is obsessed with curating his own legacy. He and his wife sit down every few years and make a 200-year plan—a plan that looks at what the world will remember them for long after they have left it. When they make this plan, they set themselves milestones for the things they want to achieve, but also the things they want to let go of.

What does this mean? For KK it's about acknowledging the parts of his history that he's hanging on to and asking whether they are still serving him. He makes an honest appraisal of how previous experiences have affected him and how they're shaping his behavior now. Then he asks himself whether they are helping or hindering him, and if they're hindering him, he sets a date for when he will let these beliefs go.

Strategy can be used not just to set goals but also to redefine ourselves. Perhaps you once worked for a company that wanted to be seen as innovative but nobody working there could stop talking about the time an innovation had failed. Imagine what it would be like to simply set a date on which that fact was no longer relevant. After all, our memory is naturally selective, so why wouldn't we use that skill to select only the parts that help us? Use your strategy as a way of keeping what serves you and letting go of the rest.

Still looking for ways to let go of the past? Check out Thordis Elva and Tom Stranger's talk on forgiveness (page 156).

AUGUST 2200

		1	2	3	4	5
6	7	8	9	10	11	12
13	14	15	16	17	18	19
20	21	22	23	24	25	26
27	28	29 ✗	30	31		

> **YOU KNOW, WE CARRY SO MUCH BAGGAGE, FROM OUR PARENTS, FROM OUR SOCIETY, FROM SO MANY PEOPLE— FEARS, INSECURITIES— AND OUR 200-YEAR PLAN REALLY LISTS ALL OUR CHILDHOOD PROBLEMS THAT WE HAVE TO EXPIRE.**
>
> **RAGHAVA KK**

Q FIND OUT MORE

Raghava KK's talk:
"What's Your 200-Year Plan?"
2012

42/100
STAND OUT

Make sure a key component of your strategy forces you to stand out.

When we have a vision, we can be very single-minded about the steps necessary to get us there.

We'll look at what our competitors have done, we'll talk to our mentors about what is necessary, and then we'll create a strategy that mimics the successes of those around us. This is a very strong starting point, but it doesn't go far enough. For a strategy to be both complete and unique, we need to ensure it features a reminder to ourselves to stand out.

In her moving and inspiring talk "From 'Devil's Child' to Star Ballerina," Michaela DePrince talks about leaving a war-torn childhood in Sierra Leone and moving to the United States with just one dream—to become a ballet dancer. She knew she would have to work hard, but she wasn't prepared to have to reveal the one thing she was most insecure about—her skin. She had been called "Devil's Child" because of her condition. Born with vitiligo, a condition that affects skin pigment, DePrince had light spots all over her torso and arms that she tried to keep covered. She soon discovered this wasn't going to be possible as a ballet dancer, and she had to let the fear of showing her true self go.

Often we can use an official strategy to hide the parts of ourselves we feel insecure about. We tell ourselves that showing a weakness or vulnerability isn't part of our success strategy. But often it ends up being our most important asset—it's what makes us stand out from the crowd.

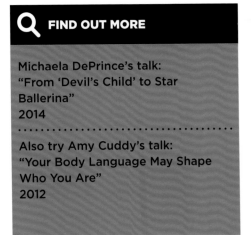

Q FIND OUT MORE

Michaela DePrince's talk: "From 'Devil's Child' to Star Ballerina"
2014

Also try Amy Cuddy's talk: "Your Body Language May Shape Who You Are"
2012

"
I WANT TO ENCOURAGE
YOUNG PEOPLE TO
ASPIRE TO DREAM.
I WANT PEOPLE TO
UNDERSTAND THAT IT'S
OK TO BE DIFFERENT;
IT'S OK TO STAND OUT.
I'M DIFFERENT.
MICHAELA DEPRINCE "

43/100
IS IT WORKING?

Don't follow your strategy blindly, but continually ask, "What do we want to achieve?" Then check your results against this.

To say that the FBI has created more terrorists than it has stopped is a controversial statement. Yet in his talk "How this FBI Strategy is Actually Creating More US-based Terrorists," which has been viewed more than a million times, Trevor Aaronson explains just why we should all be doubtful of the FBI's claim that it has foiled thousands of terror attacks. Looking at some of the organization's most high profile arrests, Aaronson shows how the desire to be seen to be catching the bad guys has led the FBI to create a strategy that actually helps would-be terrorists pursue their goals.

Of course, the original vision for the FBI wasn't to create more terrorists; it was to stop terrorism. But what Aaronson's talk highlights is how easily a strategy can get away from the original vision. By creating a strategy whose aim was to create high-profile arrests, the FBI changed its key goal. It was no longer about preventing crime, but about being seen to prevent crime—a subtle distinction.

When you're working on the strategy to support your vision, look for the ways in which it could be derailed. How could your team interpret it differently for you? What hidden benefits might your strategy reveal that could lure you away from your original

> **THE FBI IS RESPONSIBLE FOR MORE TERRORISM PLOTS IN THE UNITED STATES THAN ANY OTHER ORGANIZATION.**
> **TREVOR AARONSON**

goal? As a leader, your job is to use your strategy as a vehicle to take you to the end goal. You have to be the person that pulls back when it seems you're going down a different route—no matter how much glory there is in it.

As part of your strategy, set regular checkpoints where you step back from the day-to-day work and look at whether you're moving toward or away from your original vision. And if you're moving away from it, ask yourself, "Is this really the direction I want to go in?"

 **FIND OUT MORE**

Trevor Aaronson's talk: "How this FBI Strategy is Actually Creating More US-based Terrorists" 2015

44/100
TEST, TEST, TEST

If you really want to change the world, you need to build a test-and-fail stage into your strategy.

When Ashton Cofer and his science team decided to find a way to make supposedly unrecyclable Styrofoam recyclable, everyone thought they were joking. After all, they were kids working on a school science project. How could they possibly achieve something that no one else had? Well, spoiler alert, they did, and they received funding to file a full patent on their project so they can continue to develop it.

In the process of trying to find a way to make the unrecyclable recyclable, Cofer and his team did something scientists are familiar with but others among us might not be aware of. They proved that in order to succeed, you first have to fail—in fact, sometimes you have to fail repeatedly. These repeated failures didn't discourage Cofer, because he had already accepted them as a part of the process—the failures were necessary in order to reach a

successful conclusion. He and his team members had built failure into their strategy.

When designing your strategy, allow time and space to play. When we have a plan that doesn't allow for any failure or redesign, we're pushing ourselves into a dead end. If we are too rigid in this way, then we don't allow for learning and development, both of which are critical to success. And building in time to fail teaches your team members that it's safe to do so, allowing them to bring their most creative ideas to the table.

Q FIND OUT MORE

Ashton Cofer's talk:
"A Plan to Recycle the Unrecyclable" 2016

Also try Raphael Rose's talk:
"How Failure Cultivates Resilience" 2018

EMBRACE COMPLEXITY

Too much data can feel overwhelming but there's a simple technique to break it down.

In today's world of big data, it can often feel as though we know too much. If you've ever asked for a situation analysis, only to be faced with what seems like an infinite amount of data points, it can be tempting to decide to focus on just one or two of them. But in his talk "Simplifying Complexity," Eric Berlow argues that instead of running away from all the data, we should relax into it.

Berlow suggests a simple method for extracting the key issues from a mass of data. First, identify the key problem you want to influence—the example he uses is popular support for the Afghan government. Next, look at the data sets that are up to three degrees removed from the issue. (You'll soon see that beyond this

it becomes tricky to influence the data.) This then gives you the key areas you can effectively influence—the data points you can concentrate on.

While it can be tempting to dive into all the data, take a step back and look for the areas you can actually influence. Creating patterns of influence and working through them one by one, rather than trying to change everything, allows us to create a strategy that feels achievable rather than overwhelming. By embracing the complexity of the data, you can use it to help you identify your key priorities.

FIND OUT MORE

Eric Berlow's talk:
"Simplifying Complexity"
2010

46/100
GO AGAINST THE GRAIN

You don't have to have a completely new answer to a problem. Instead, you can just approach it from a different angle.

Innovation isn't always about inventing something new or a new way of doing things. Sometimes it's about looking at a problem from a slightly different angle," explains Jeff Kozak in his talk "Lessons from a Former Air Force Pilot on Counterintuitive Thinking."

When you're trying to solve a problem innovatively, first ask yourself, "What do we usually do in this situation?" Then ask, "What would we do if we knew our usual response was not the optimal one?" So often we get used to doing things in the way they've always been done. And then when someone asks us why we do them like that, we reply, "Because that's the way they're done." If you truly want to create something innovative in your market, start by going against traditional wisdom.

For Kozak, looking at problems from a different angle allows him to create new strategies, ones that might previously have been overlooked because they go against traditional thinking. When you're putting together your strategy, make sure to ask yourself, "What is the counterintuitive answer here?" Challenge yourself to solve the problem without using any of the traditional solutions or with severe restrictions in place. Go past your first answer and challenge the convention. And remember, if you catch yourself reaching for the standard response to the problem, you might find an answer but it won't be an innovative one.

If you need help being brave to do things differently, read Geena Rocero's talk on breaking through belief systems (page 100) or Daniel Lismore's talk on being your own masterpiece (page 140).

Q FIND OUT MORE

Jeff Kozak's talk:
"Lessons from a Former Air Force Pilot on Counterintuitive Thinking"
2017

"INNOVATORS DON'T SEE DIFFERENT THINGS; THEY SEE THINGS DIFFERENTLY."

JEFF KOZAK

DON'T IGNORE THE RHINO

Whatever you do, make sure your strategy doesn't ignore a preventable danger just because it seems too big.

A term long used by strategists for the rare, unforeseeable but also unavoidable danger that you simply cannot prepare for is "the black swan." But Michele Wucker believes this metaphor has allowed policy makers to hide behind a reality—often we can predict these black swans, but we are just choosing not to.

When we look back in history at large-scale crises, we can often see a clear line between the events that happened before them and the crises themselves. Using the 2008 financial crash as an example, Wucker points out that the rapid increase in house prices beforehand should have been a clear indication that the bubble would have to pop at some point—but everyone ignored the signs. She calls this willful ignorance "the gray rhino." We should be able to see it, but somehow we don't.

If you want to see the gray rhinos, then you have to be open to seeing things you might not like or agree with. You also need to accept that some of these gray rhinos might feel impossible to influence, such as climate change. But the reality is that we can all make some small changes.

When we seek out information, share this information with others, and truly open our eyes to the gray rhinos, we give ourselves the power to tackle them. What are the gray rhinos in your strategy? What information have you ignored because the problem seems too big or doesn't fit the narrative you want to tell? These are your gray rhinos. Open your eyes to them now.

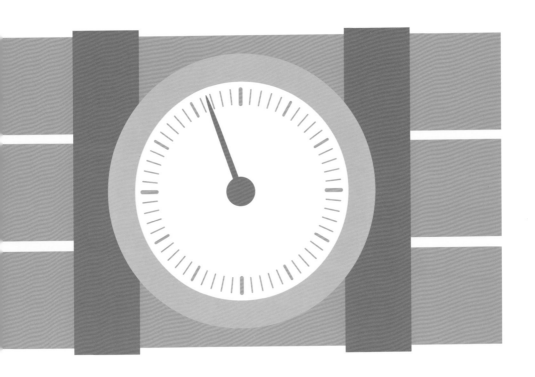

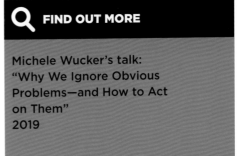

> **THE PEOPLE WHO ARE WILLING TO RECOGNIZE THE PROBLEMS AROUND THEM AND MAKE PLANS ARE THE ONES WHO ARE ABLE TO TOLERATE MORE RISK.**
> **MICHELE WUCKER**

FIND OUT MORE

Michele Wucker's talk: "Why We Ignore Obvious Problems—and How to Act on Them" 2019

BE BRAVE and ask for help

Being a leader means being the person who stands at the front of the pack and faces down the enemy. In this chapter, we look at how we muster the courage to stand our ground when faced with adversity, what it really means to be brave, and how leaders can encourage others to be bold too.

THE POWER OF GROWTH

By developing a growth mind-set, we can adapt and learn rather than expecting to have all the answers right now.

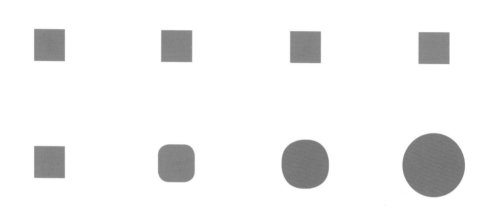

Do you believe in the human ability to grow and adapt? Carol Dweck does. She has dedicated her life to researching human growth and in particular why some people have what she calls a "growth mind-set"— the belief that even if they don't know or can't do something right now, they will be able to in the future.

Dweck encountered growth mind-set early on in her career when she looked at how a group of young children responded to a challenge. Some of them lapped it up, but others were put off by the difficulty of the task she set. The kids who loved a challenge had a growth mind-set—they could process the fact that they weren't capable of meeting the challenge right now but believed that they could learn and adapt, and would one day have the ability to take it on.

Bravery is not something we are born with, but something we grow into and learn as we progress through life. However, it is much harder to be brave if we believe that the person we are now is the same person we will always be.

A growth mind-set is the thing that allows us to be brave in the face of adversity. It's our brain's way of

" INSTEAD OF LUXURIATING IN THE POWER OF YET, THEY WERE GRIPPED IN THE TYRANNY OF NOW. "

CAROL DWECK

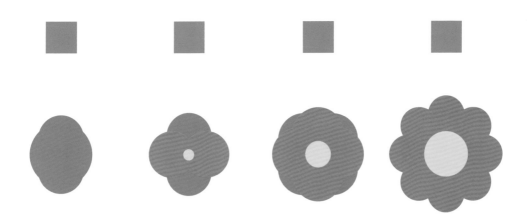

encouraging us to love a challenge—here's a chance to learn! When we look at adversity not as something scary or demeaning but as an opportunity to learn, we diminish the fears it brings with it and start to feel excited. We take on the power of "not yet"—Dweck's idea that while we might not know what to do yet, we will in the future.

FIND OUT MORE

Carol Dweck's talk:
"The Power of Believing That You Can Improve"
2014

SHOW THE SCARS

Being a leader doesn't mean you have to hide the scars you've gained on the way to the top.

Eman Mohammed is a female photojournalist in Gaza. In Palestinian culture, it's a career that isn't considered appropriate for a woman, and she spent most of the early part of her working life dealing not only with threats to her safety from the war waging around her, but also from her colleagues.

One day, she met Mohammed Khader, a man whose house had been razed to the ground. All that was left was the bath he used to wash his kids in. So, he dragged the bath to the top of the rubble and continued to give his children their daily wash. Mohammed photographed Khader doing this, and in the process she realized that being brave isn't about hiding how our history has affected us but about being able to acknowledge it.

As leaders, we all have moments in our history when we have fought battles and lost, when we have been scarred or damaged because of the circumstances we found ourselves in. Bravery in leadership is not about hiding these scars but about showing them off. When we are open about the problems we've faced, we give our team the opportunity to see us in our full humanity and to be inspired by us. Think of the people you look to for inspiration, then ask yourself how many of them have lived perfect lives.

In order to let others know you have been through your own challenges, you need to drag the bathtub on top of the rubble.

For more brave authenticity check out Morgana Bailey's talk on coming out in the workplace (page 141).

Q FIND OUT MORE

Eman Mohammed's talk:
"The Courage to Tell a Hidden Story"
2014

Also try Tarana Burke's talk:
"Me Too Is a Movement, Not a Moment"
2018

SPREAD THE BRAVERY

Just as fear can be contagious, so can courage. When we take bold actions, we pass that bravery on to others.

Have you ever been on a flight when turbulence kicks in and it gets a bit rocky? You look toward the flight attendants, and if they look calm, you feel instantly reassured. If there's a twitch of nervousness, however, you start to panic. Both courage and fear are contagious, and Damon Davis experienced this in an extreme manner.

When Michael Brown Jr. was gunned down in Ferguson in 2014, Davis went to join the protests that took place in the wake of his death. Standing on the streets facing down armed police, he could feel the fear in the crowd but he could also feel the courage. And it was this courage that gave him the bravery to bring the campaign into his work and start making art around it.

When we do something brave, it's often in the knowledge that we won't be alone— our bravery is the impetus that others need in order to act. Part of being a great leader is understanding that when we are brave we might feel like we are the only one daring to stand apart from the crowd, but that slowly our bravery will inspire those around us and we'll be leading a revolution. Of course, the opposite is also true: if we're afraid and we show it, we run the risk of spreading that fear to our team and colleagues. So, before you tell others how you're feeling, think about how you want them to feel and then see if you can spread that instead.

Q FIND OUT MORE

Damon Davis's talk:
"Courage Is Contagious"
2017

I THINK WE SHOULD BE CONVEYORS OF COURAGE IN THE WORK THAT WE DO.

DAMON DAVIS

51/100
BREAK THROUGH BELIEFS

As we grow up, we take on the beliefs of our parents, our teachers, and society around us. Leaders are brave enough to challenge these beliefs.

One of the hardest things to do is to go against our family or our community. When Geena Rocero came out to her community as a transgender woman, she went against all the beliefs she had been brought up with. And when she moved from the Philippines to the United States, she did so knowing that she would still have to stand up to the community around her. The suicide rate for trans people is nine times higher than average—it takes a lot of courage to be able to face down daily hate and stigma.

Rocero epitomizes the power that comes from standing up for what we believe even when it goes against the societal mores of our community. When we own our own truth, we start to influence and change the culture around us—we become the instigators of change rather than the recipients of it. But how do we go about confronting the beliefs of our society?

For Rocero there were two stages to the process. The first was to own who she was and what she believed in unashamedly, and to share this with those around her. When we are vulnerable with those closest to us, we give them a chance to accept us, rewarding our bravery. The second stage is finding others who have been similarly brave and who stand for the things we do. Rocero found her community in New York. Where will you find yours?

Q FIND OUT MORE

Geena Rocero's talk:
"Why I Must Come Out"
2014

Also try Cleo Wade's talk:
"Want to Change the World? Start by Being Brave Enough to Care"
2017

SOME PEOPLE HAVE THE COURAGE TO BREAK FREE, NOT TO ACCEPT THE LIMITATIONS IMPOSED BY THE COLOR OF THEIR SKIN OR BY THE BELIEFS OF THOSE THAT SURROUND THEM. THOSE PEOPLE ARE ALWAYS THE THREAT TO THE STATUS QUO.

GEENA ROCERO

CHALLENGE YOUR AUDIENCE

Be brave enough to tell people the things they don't want to hear.

In her talk "Change Your Channel," Mallence Bart-Williams hits her audience with some hard home truths and repeatedly confounds their expectations. She is talking to a Western audience and she wants to challenge the beliefs they have about her home, Sierra Leone, and Africa as a whole. She starts by telling them she wants to talk about the richest continent in the world, assuming they'll think she means North America, then she tells them she wants to talk about Africa. She explains why the advertising they see urging charity donations to Africa is "charity porn." You can see the looks of discomfort on the faces of those seated before her, but Bart-Williams doesn't allow this to stop her from spreading her message.

It takes a lot of bravery to tell your truth to people who don't want to hear it, but it's a mark of Bart-Williams's ability as a leader that not only can she do this but

she can also bring her audience with her. Her refusal to soften the blow for them sends a message of "take it or leave it," and it encourages people to sit up and take note of what she has to say.

When was the last time you stood up and delivered bad news? It can be scary and uncomfortable. As humans, our instinct is to want to be liked by those around us, but truly brave leaders know that if we want to make change, sometimes we have to deliver the cold, unpalatable truth.

🔍 FIND OUT MORE

Mallence Bart-Williams's talk:
"Change Your Channel"
2015

IT'S SUPER-SWEET OF YOU TO COME WITH YOUR COLORED PAPER IN EXCHANGE FOR OUR GOLD AND DIAMONDS. BUT INSTEAD YOU SHOULD COME EMPTY HANDED FILLED WITH INTEGRITY AND HONOUR.

MALLENCE BART-WILLIAMS

BRAVERY BEATS PERFECTION

Take a big leap. Even if you don't get it quite right, bravery will carry you further than a leap—perfect but small.

"Most girls are taught to avoid risk and failure," says Reshma Saujani. "We're taught to smile pretty, play it safe, get all As. Boys, on the other hand, are taught to play rough, swing high, crawl to the top of the monkey bars, and then jump off headfirst."

In this powerful opening to her talk "Teach Girls Bravery, Not Perfection," Saujani neatly illustrates the training we need when young in order to strengthen our bravery muscles. If we're going to practice bravery when we're older, then we have to stop striving for perfection and instead get things wrong a few times. If we're so worried about getting things right that we never step outside our comfort zone, then we'll never push ourselves.

Failure is an inevitable part of success, so we need to get comfortable with the idea that sometimes the work we produce will be below par or simply not good enough at all. While Saujani's research found that this was a gendered issue, the way to solve it is the same whether you're male or female.

First, we have to make sure that the success or failure isn't personal. Saujani explains that when boys are struggling to make something work, they think the problem lies outside of them, while girls think it's their own fault—and the first of these is the easier to process. So, the next time you're faced with a difficult problem, ask yourself what or who else besides you could be making it challenging.

> # IT OFTEN TAKES MANY, MANY TRIES UNTIL THAT MAGICAL MOMENT WHEN WHAT YOU'RE TRYING TO BUILD COMES TO LIFE. IT REQUIRES PERSEVERANCE. IT REQUIRES IMPERFECTION.
>
> **RESHMA SAUJANI**

Second, we need to be proud of the process. Show people your work along the way, rather than just at the end. It takes bravery to allow people to see the imperfections in our work, but when we do so we also boost the muscle that makes us brave. In this case, practicing imperfection really does make perfect.

🔍 FIND OUT MORE

Reshma Saujani's talk:
"Teach Girls Bravery, Not Perfection"
2016

Also try Raphael Rose's talk:
"How Failure Cultivates Resilience"
2018

CONTROL YOUR FOCUS

When you find yourself anxious about a big event, focus your attention on the moments before it rather than on the event itself.

Why would people take part in a sport that could kill them? Free diving has been a sport for hundreds of years and it requires incredible bravery. Most of us can't do it because it becomes very uncomfortable very quickly, and most of us give up when the level of discomfort gets too much.

In his talk "Bravery Begins with Belief," sports psychologist Ant Williams teaches us to muster our bravery by taking our attention away from the thing we're about to do and instead putting it on the moment before. He gives the example of free diving. The scary part about this sport is being underwater, unable to breathe. So, rather than putting our attention on where our fear is, we put it at T minus 1, the moment just before. For free divers, this means concentrating on everything that will happen just before they enter the water. They do this by focusing on control of their breathing and on their conviction that they will go through with the dive.

If you're facing a situation that scares you, try moving your attention away from the situation itself and put it at T minus 1. If your team has a big presentation, for example, focus on the preparation for it, not on the presentation itself. As a leader, you can encourage those around you to do the same—put your focus on the moment just before the big event and feel your courage grow.

There are more tips on focus in David Blaine's talk on freediving (page 10) and Minda Dentler's talk on overcoming adversity (page 13).

FIND OUT MORE

Ant Williams's talk:
"Bravery Begins with Belief"
2014

RISK TAKERS DO SOMETHING DIFFERENT TO THE REST OF US—THEY LEARN HOW TO MANAGE THEIR FEAR, AND IN THE PROCESS THEY BUILD CONFIDENCE.

ANT WILLIAMS

CONFRONT YOUR FEARS

When we take a good look at the experiences that shaped us, we start to see who we really are and what matters.

Joshua Prager was in a car crash at age 19 that left him paralyzed down one side of his body. It took him years to learn to walk again, and he spent most of his college career in a wheelchair. For decades, Prager thought about the man who had caused the crash—and then one day he set out to find him.

When Prager finally came face to face with the man whose bad driving had injured him, he expected him to be remorseful. He went to meet him so that he could hear him say the words "I'm sorry." Instead, however, the man showed minimal remorse and saw the crash as an act of God. It was during this meeting that Prager realized that the bravest thing we can do as humans is to acknowledge our own weaknesses and failures.

How we behave as leaders sets the cultural tone throughout any organization we find ourselves working in. If we are brave enough to admit our own mistakes and failings, we set a standard for those around us to live up to. Instead of creating a world where we blame others for the problems we've created, we take responsibility for our actions and encourage others to do the same. It's very easy to say, "I did well," and very hard to say, "I screwed up"—admitting our faults takes bravery. But when we do so, we clearly show up as a leader.

Q FIND OUT MORE

Joshua Prager's talk:
"In Search of the Man Who Broke My Neck"
2013

Also try Tim Ferriss's talk:
"Smash Fear, Learn Anything"
2008

ANYONE CAN BE BRAVE

While bravery is a trait of leadership, it's not a trait found in all leaders. Sometimes we have to look further down the ladder to find the bravest people.

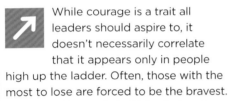

While courage is a trait all leaders should aspire to, it doesn't necessarily correlate that it appears only in people high up the ladder. Often, those with the most to lose are forced to be the bravest.

When Chetna Gala Sinha first met Kantabai, the woman who would inspire her to open her very own bank, Kantabai was living in terrible circumstances. She was working as blacksmith, but she was desperate to save some money so she could buy a plastic sheet to cover her family when it rained. The bank refused to offer Kantabai a savings account, so Sinha applied for a banking license in order to start a bank for women like Kantabai. However, her license was refused.

When Sinha returned to her village, the women there told her to stop crying and sort the problem out. The license had been refused because too few of them knew how to read and write, so they decided to learn. And they also decided they would march to the banking authorities and show them that they could certainly work out the interest on a loan faster than anyone who worked there.

This determination in the face of adversity shows the sort of courage that can be found when people have nothing to lose. As leaders, we can tap into this by reminding ourselves of a time when we, too, had nothing to lose, when we didn't have a title or reputation to worry about. What would we have done then?

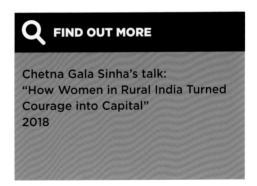

Q FIND OUT MORE

Chetna Gala Sinha's talk: "How Women in Rural India Turned Courage into Capital" 2018

ENCOURAGE OTHERS

Our role as leaders is not just to step into our own bravery, but also to encourage those around us to step into theirs.

When Khalida Brohi started a campaign to raise awareness of honor killings in her home of Pakistan, people around the world praised her for her bravery. Her actions meant that she came under threat from the local community, and her family were sent abusive letters and their property was attacked. People told her she was brave to stand up to all of this, but Brohi couldn't understand why it was happening—after all, she was trying to do something good for her community.

However, when she looked back at the campaign, Brohi realized she had failed to do one very important thing. She had started a campaign to help women threatened with honor killings, but she hadn't involved them in the campaign— she hadn't asked them what would help or how they would feel about it.

Brohi went back to those communities, but this time with an apology for not supporting them properly and with a desire to work with them as opposed to for them. What she found was that all people needed in order to believe they could step forward and lead the campaign with her was for her to tell them they could. By pointing out their bravery and achievements, she gave them the courage to step forward and own them. By being brave enough to admit that she had failed, Brohi brought out the bravery in others.

Q FIND OUT MORE

Khalida Brohi's talk:
"How I Work to Protect Women from Honor Killings"
2014

I TRULY BELIEVE, TO CREATE WOMEN LEADERS, THERE'S ONLY ONE THING YOU HAVE TO DO: JUST LET THEM KNOW THAT THEY HAVE WHAT IT TAKES TO BE A LEADER.

KHALIDA BROHI

BUILD BRIDGES

Your unique experiences will allow you to build bridges between different worlds.

They say that getting old is not for the weak, but in her talk "The Power of Aging," Ariane van de Ven tries to break down some of the myths about aging. She shows a video of her eighty-year-old father fencing with a man half his age, and she talks about how by 2050 the number of people aged over 65 will have tripled. You can feel the discomfort in the audience. Getting old and dying are not things we want to think about, much less talk about.

Part of being brave is being really honest with ourselves about our future. As leaders in the workplace, we can extend this to be honest about the future of our marketplace or industry. By talking about aging, Van de Ven forces us not just to be leaders in the workplace, but also in our own lives. She challenges us to look into the future and think about what we want to find when we get there.

Van de Ven talks about Patty Moore, a designer who at twenty-five dressed up and behaved as though she were an old woman, to help her understand the needs old people have. Moore described the experience as incredibly scary. The reality is that as a leader you will sometimes be looking at a future that doesn't look good for your team or your industry. You can choose to ignore it, but actually confronting the worst possible scenarios and planning for them brings you power over them.

Sometimes facing up to our future can be terrifying—there may be things we can't predict or control. But we need to take a page out of Van de Ven's father's book and make a conscious decision about how we want our old age to look. Do we want to be light on our feet and still fencing? If so, we need to start planning now.

Q FIND OUT MORE

Ariane van de Ven's talk:
"The Power of Aging"
2014

Also try Michele Wucker's talk:
"Why We Ignore Obvious Problems—and How to Act on Them"
2019

I WANT TO LOOK FORWARD TO BEING A SUPER-COOL SEVENTY-FIVE, EIGHTY-YEAR-OLD WOMAN THAT EVERYBODY THINKS KICKS ASS.

ARIANE VAN DE VEN

BE COLLABORATIVE
with your team, your customers, and even your competitors

Too often we link leadership with winning, but in today's culture, collaboration and letting go of the win/lose mentality are more important than ever. This chapter looks at some of the great achievements that couldn't have happened without collaboration and explains how to facilitate it.

59/100
SHARE WIDELY

Don't be afraid to put what you know out there. The competitive advantage gained through collaboration is greater than when you operate in secrecy.

When Pardis Sabeti found herself on the front line of the Ebola outbreak in Sierra Leone, she knew that she wasn't going to be able to solve the problem in the traditional manner. She had been collecting data from the blood samples of victims of the disease, but analyzing it was going to take far too long. Rather than working by herself, Sarbeti took a risky decision: she published the data on the web. "We just released it to the whole world and said, 'Help us.' And help came."

Sarbeti could have kept the data to herself. Yes, it would have taken her much longer to analyze it, but when she did she could then have published a paper on it and been the first to discuss her findings—she could have kept all the glory for herself. But as leaders, we need to know when is the right time to hold on to our power and when we will get further by sharing it.

By releasing her data, Sarbeti invited in some of the world's leading virus trackers. In doing so, she suddenly had access to skills and expertise that would have eluded her had she kept those data secret. Working with others in this way, she could find a solution and implement it much faster, saving countless lives. The benefits far outweighed the loss of exclusivity, and in sacrificing her own gain for others, Pardis showed true leadership.

FIND OUT MORE

Pardis Sarbeti's talk:
"How We'll Fight the Next Deadly Virus"
2015
. . . .
Also try James Curleigh's talk:
"How to Enhance and Expand a Global Brand"
2013

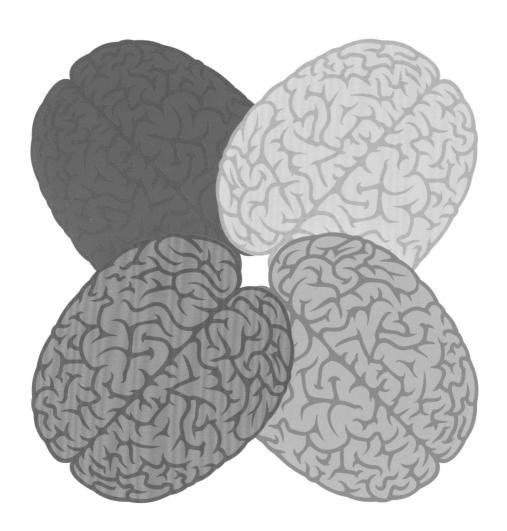

 LET US NOT LET THE WORLD BE DEFINED BY THE DESTRUCTION WROUGHT BY ONE VIRUS, BUT ILLUMINATED BY BILLIONS OF HEARTS AND MINDS WORKING IN UNITY. 🙶

PARDIS SABETI

IN ON THE JOKE

There's no bonding experience quite like the one when you realize you and a few others are in on a joke no one else knows.

Have you ever sat on the subway and wondered why the man opposite you isn't wearing pants?

If you live in a big city, you might just dismiss him as yet another crazy guy, but in reality you might find you're part of a sketch scene created by Improv Everywhere.

In his talk "The Shared Experience of Absurdity," Charlie Todd describes how, back in 2002, Improv Everywhere started the now annual "no-pants subway ride"— a day in January when people ride the subway without any pants on. The first time the group did it, just seven of them took part, and they filmed the reactions of the people on the subway around them. When they watched the film back, they realized that their audience had created a little group. As each person noticed the no-pants brigade, they felt slightly uncomfortable, but when they caught the eye of another regular commuter and realized they were having the same experience, they felt like they were part of something. Realizing that they were in on a joke bonded an entire subway car of strangers.

As leaders, we are wary of creating cliques among our teams as we want everyone to feel included. But your team can bond if they feel they are a part of something that no one on the outside quite understands. This might be the terminology you use among yourselves, or eating lunch at the same spot every Friday. Whatever it is, just make sure that you let anyone new in on the joke when they join the team.

Want to bring some humor into your office (while keeping your pants on)? Check out Kasha Patel's talk on the power of comedy (page 54).

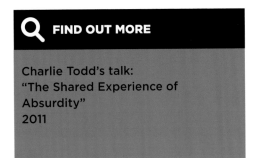

🔍 FIND OUT MORE

Charlie Todd's talk:
"The Shared Experience of Absurdity"
2011

BE MUTUALLY RELIANT

Look to collaborate with people who, in the pursuit of their own goal, will help you with yours.

Can you think of a personal experience about ants? Scientist Kirsti Abbott believes that everyone has a story about ants. Whether it's ants stealing food from a summer picnic or giving us a nip when we nearly stand on them.

Abbott had a negative view of ants until she spent three years on Christmas Island, a place where the brilliantly named yellow crazy ants congregate in such numbers that the ground looks like it's covered in an ant carpet. She had to modify how she worked and lived to cope with the ants, and says she had to become Zen in order to deal with them. But Abbott did discover something interesting about the ants. They formed an alliance with sap-sucking insects living in the island's trees. The insects eat the tree sap and excrete honeydew, which the ants then feed on. The ants know they need the insects in order to survive and so protect them, and in turn the insects reward the ants for their protection. Even though the two groups are not related, they are mutually reliant and have created a system that works for both of them.

Often we look to collaborate with those who are like us. However, by searching out groups with different goals, we might be able to find people on whom we can be mutually reliant, who won't be competing with us, and who might just help us change the ecosystem around us.

> **[ANTS] CAN HELP YOU CONNECT TO THE EARTH, YOUR EARTH, OUR EARTH. AND HELP YOU APPRECIATE THE LITTLE THINGS THAT ARE RUNNING THE WORLD.**
> **KIRSTI ABBOTT**

Q FIND OUT MORE

Kirsti Abbott's talk: "The Ants That Run the World" 2016

62/100
HUMILITY BREEDS COLLABORATION

If you want to lead a truly collaborative team, the first thing you need to do is put down your own ego.

How does a leader transform a group of complete strangers into a team? In her 2017 talk on this subject, Amy Edmondson uses the idea of "teaming" or "teamwork on the fly" to show how it's done.

In 2010, when thirty-three Chilean miners were trapped underground with very little food and no real plan for how to get them out, it seemed like their chances of survival were minimal. When she studied the rescue attempt, Edmondson noticed three key values that made the rescue team incredibly collaborative. For a start, the members of the team were all humble—completing the mission was more important than being the person who had the idea. Second, they were curious, asking questions about each other's experience and fully listening to the answers. And third, they were free to take risks because their culture of collaboration meant that failure wasn't seen as losing to someone else but as trying to find a solution.

Most importantly, for teaming to work it needs leaders who are clear that they don't have the answer, who are happy to admit that the other members of the team might know more than them, and who understand that on this occasion their job is to extract the information rather than provide it. Teaming requires a level of humility that is present only in truly great leaders.

The Chilean operation lasted sixty-nine days, but eventually every single miner was rescued.

Q FIND OUT MORE

Amy Edmondson's talk:
"How to Turn a Group of Strangers into a Team"
2017
. . . .
Also try Charlie Todd's talk:
"The Shared Experience of Absurdity"
2011

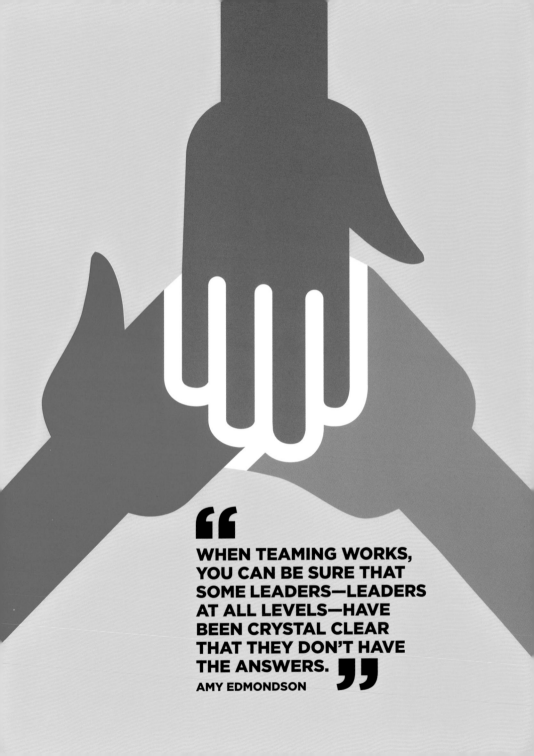

" WHEN TEAMING WORKS, YOU CAN BE SURE THAT SOME LEADERS—LEADERS AT ALL LEVELS—HAVE BEEN CRYSTAL CLEAR THAT THEY DON'T HAVE THE ANSWERS. "

AMY EDMONDSON

RELATIONAL EQUITY

For collaboration to work, we all need to play an equal part in it.

> **COMMUNITY AND POLICING: WE'VE ALL LOST THAT PRECIOUS GIFT, AND I CALL IT RELATIONAL EQUITY. WE'VE LOST IT WITH ONE ANOTHER. IT'S NOT SOMEBODY ELSE'S FAULT—IT'S ALL OF OUR FAULT.**
>
> **MELVIN RUSSELL**

Melvin Russell is a policeman, a preacher, and a black man. He is part of several different, diverse communities, each of which plays an important part in his life. And yet, as he continued his career in the police, Russell started to see how the links between his communities had begun to break down. So, he decided to do something about it.

Rather than retiring as he had intended, Russell worked his way up through the police ranks and ended up as a district commander in Baltimore, looking after one of the most disenfranchised communities in the United States. When he looked at how he could rebuild the links between the police and the community, he soon realized that there had been a lack of responsibility on both sides.

First, Russell had the police department focus on its role in the breakdown and how this could be fixed. He encouraged the police officers to treat citizens with more respect, to spend more time out in the community, and to start serving the community as well as protecting it. In the second part of his talk, Russell also relates how the community had to step up and look after itself as well. He describes the actions at play here as "relational equality."

In other words, if we're going to work together, then all sides have to put in equal amounts of effort.

If you start to see cracks appearing in your team, look to see whether one side might be picking up too much of the slack or going beyond their remit. Is there relational equality among those who work for you? Is everyone doing their fair share and supporting those around them? Without this, collaboration and trust break down. As a leader, it's your duty to do as Melvin did and call it out when you see it.

FIND OUT MORE

Melvin Russell's talk:
"I Love Being a Police Officer but We Need Reform"
2015

LOVE YOUR NEIGHBOR

Sometimes we find ourselves collaborating with people we might not like, but remembering to treat them as though they are our neighbor can help.

When Michael Tubbs was elected the youngest ever mayor of a United States city with a population of more than 100,000, he knew that he had to change community relations radically if he wanted his district to improve.

Tubbs remembered the parable of the Good Samaritan in the Bible—a man lies bleeding at the side of the road and several people walk past him, until one man, who is supposed to be his enemy, stops and helps him. What Tubbs took

from this is that our job as a good neighbor is to recognize when people in our community need help and to give them that help whether we like them or not. Because when we lift them up, we lift up the entire neighborhood.

Tubbs explains how this is working in his city: "So for the past three years, we've been working on two strategies, ceasefire and advance peace, where we give these guys as much attention, as much love from social services, from opportunities, from tattoo removals, in some cases even cash,

> **WHEN WE SEE SOMEONE DIFFERENT FROM US, THEY SHOULD NOT REFLECT OUR FEARS, OUR ANXIETIES, OUR INSECURITIES, THE PREJUDICES WE'VE BEEN TAUGHT, OUR BIASES—BUT WE SHOULD SEE OURSELVES. WE SHOULD SEE OUR COMMON HUMANITY.**
>
> **MICHAEL TUBBS**

as a gift from law enforcement. And last year, we saw a 40 percent reduction in homicides and a 30 percent reduction in violent crime."

When we have a difficult team member, it can be easy to assume the best thing to do is to get rid of them. But if we can find a way to lift them up, then we provide the sort of leadership that advances both them and the whole of the team.

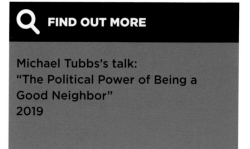

🔍 FIND OUT MORE

Michael Tubbs's talk:
"The Political Power of Being a Good Neighbor"
2019

THE GENERATION GAP

How do you get members of different generations to work as a team? By treating them as individuals.

> **" MEET PEOPLE IN THEIR ONLYNESS; THAT IS, THAT SPOT IN THE WORLD WHERE ONLY WE STAND, AS A FUNCTION OF OUR UNIQUE HISTORY, OUR EXPERIENCES, AND OUR HOPES. BUT THIS REQUIRES FLEXIBILITY AND CURIOSITY. "**
>
> **LEAH GEORGES**

For the first time in history, we have five generations of people all living and working together—from those born before the Second World War to Generation Z, those just coming into the workplace now. And the values and attitudes of these generations seem vastly different. So how, as leaders, do we unite individuals who not only seem to disagree on what's important, but increasingly appear to hold each other in very low regard?

Well, the good news, says Leah Georges, is that those generational stereotypes might not actually exist. Her research into generational stereotypes has shown that even if the generations themselves do exist—and she's not convinced that they do—the stereotypes about them are different depending on where you are in the world. Add to this the problem of confirmation bias (meaning that when we hear a stereotype about ourselves we are then more likely to live up to it), and it starts to become apparent that we might be worrying about the wrong thing.

Instead, Georges suggests that we meet people exactly where they are. We ask them questions about their values and beliefs, what they enjoy doing outside of the office, and what makes work meaningful for them, and then we tailor our approach to them accordingly.

When leaders start buying into stereotypes, we run the risk of making

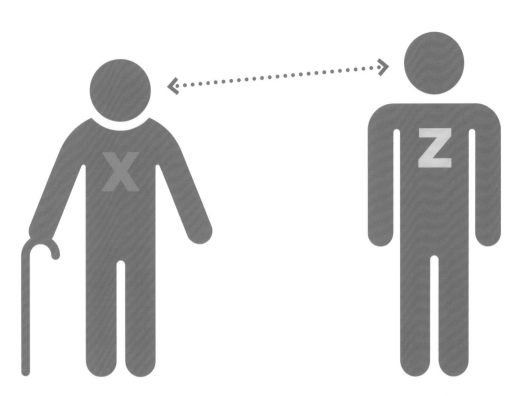

assumptions about our teams. We assume they'll want more time off or that they won't be able to handle a difficult project. We assume they won't know how to use digital technology or that their age makes them exactly the right person to run our social media accounts. All of this is sloppy leadership, because we're not taking the time to work out exactly what makes our team members tick.

The next time you assume a millennial really enjoys avocado toast for breakfast, check your assumptions and check with them first.

🔍 FIND OUT MORE

Leah Georges's talk:
"How Generational Stereotypes Hold Us Back at Work"
2018

Also try Clay Shirky's talk:
"Institutions vs. Collaboration"
2005

COLLECTIVE GENIUS

Moments of innovation require leaders to bring everyone's individual strengths to the table and let them shine.

Do you know how many people it takes to make a Pixar movie? Roughly 250 people working over four to five years, according to Harvard professor Linda Hill in her talk on creative collaboration. And every one of those 250 people is necessary to create just one film—without even one of them, it wouldn't work.

When we think of creative genius it's very easy for us to picture "a" creative genius—just one person whose moment of inspiration changed the world. In cultural lore, creative genius is Archimedes leaping out his bathtub and shouting "Eureka!" But in today's working world, Hill explains, it's different. Creative genius occurs when we layer the creativity of individuals over each other, and it requires teamwork.

As a leader, it's important to create the right culture in order for this creative genius to flourish. That means allowing for conflict and diversity, and being able to manage these. It's your job to encourage your teams to debate and discuss ideas, but also to find resolution. You're not there to dictate but to direct, guide, and hold the

 CREATIVE ABRASION IS ABOUT BEING ABLE TO CREATE A MARKETPLACE OF IDEAS THROUGH DEBATE AND DISCOURSE. IN INNOVATIVE ORGANIZATIONS, THEY AMPLIFY DIFFERENCES, THEY DON'T MINIMIZE THEM.

LINDA HILL

space for creation and innovation. This leads to what Hill calls "creative abrasion."

In a traditional leadership of command and control, creative abrasion wouldn't be possible, but without it creative genius cannot flourish. True leaders recognize the need for debate and discussion, and are comfortable enough to be able to stand in it and find a way through.

🔍 FIND OUT MORE

Linda Hill's talk:
"How to Manage for Collective Creativity"
2014

SHARE AND SHARE ALIKE

The sharing economy has taken off. Here's how you can use this trend in the workplace.

Rachel Botsman is obsessed with what drives the new sharing economy. She thinks there are four key factors at play. The first is a reemergence of the importance of community and neighborly behavior. The second is the rise in mobile technology, making it easier for us to find things and interact with what's around us. The third is a fear for our environment. And the fourth is the global recession of 2009, which changed consumer behavior.

When we look at what these four factors tell us about human behavior, we start to see a rise in levels of concern and responsibility, wherein previous decades these were perhaps a bit quieter. There is now a desire to make the most of what we have, to rent rather than to own, and to share with those around us. This collective sense of responsibility and neighborliness harks back to the trends Melvin Russell and Michael Tubbs discuss in their talks (see pages 122 and 124).

Within the workplace it's easy to see how leaders can capitalize on these trends to increase collaboration. The rise of collaborative technology makes it easier than ever before to share ideas and heads off the traditional tendency of having just one owner per project. Culturally, encouraging your team to share work, not as a way to lose ownership of it but instead as a way to achieve the best possible outcome, taps into this spirit of collective consumption.

Q FIND OUT MORE

Rachel Botsman's talk: "The Case for Collaborative Consumption" 2010

Also try Melvin Russell's talk: "I Love Being a Police Officer but We Need Reform" 2015

COLLABORATION CAN SURPRISE

While we might think we know the answer we are looking for, collaboration opens us up to other possibilities.

When Salvatore Iaconesi was diagnosed with brain cancer, he refused to handle it in the traditional way. He found that his hospital wanted him to become a literal "patient"—meaning, as he points out, "one who waits." But he didn't have the time or the patience for this.

Instead, Iaconesi decided to change his relationship with the cancer and see what he could learn from it. He put the data about his brain cancer on the internet and asked people to send him a cure. And he didn't just mean a traditional cure. Of course, if any medical professional could get rid of the cancer that would be great, but Iaconesi also wanted to know what a musical cure would look like, or a poetic cure. He wanted to experience what the entire world felt and had to say about his cancer.

How often do we find ourselves going in just the one direction? We have a problem, we think we know what the answer should be, and so we set off to talk to the people we think will have the answer we're expecting. However, by inviting other people in, people who might not be obvious collaborators, we're opening ourselves up to new experiences and new information.

While it might be safer to go down the traditional route—to head to the doctor for a cure—leaders can set an example by reaching out and bringing in unusual collaborations. Look outside your own box and see what you can cure by seeking out the unexpected.

🔍 FIND OUT MORE

Salvatore Iaconesi's talk:
"What Happened When I Open-sourced My Brain Cancer"
2013

Also try Pardis Sarbeti's talk:
"How We'll Fight the Next Deadly Virus"
2015

69/100
DON'T BE DEFENSIVE

When our ideas are questioned, we get defensive. Here's how to defuse that defensiveness within your team.

Did you know that chickens are collaborative? In his talk "Cultivating Collaboration: Don't Be So Defensive!", Jim Tamm calls these collaborative chickens "the green zone"—there are no star performers among chickens that lay lots of eggs, but they all get along very well. In contrast, "the red zone" does have star performer chickens, but they are defensive. In fact, so defensive of their status are they that they'll peck other chickens to death to retain their status.

When scientists studied these chickens, they found that their environment determined their behavior. The effect of being put in the red zone on more timid chickens was to turn them aggressive, while more aggressive chickens put in the green zone became calmer. And it seems that this plays out in offices as well.

When we create a culture that rewards collaboration and cooperation, we actively encourage our team members to behave in that way. When we reward aggressiveness, this spreads throughout the organization like "a virus," as Tamm puts it. And while it might seem productive to create a red zone filled with star performers, eventually these individuals will be more concerned with trying to take each other out than lay eggs. Your star performers will very quickly become less than average.

So, the next time someone questions why, as a leader, you want a collaborative team over an aggressive one, remind them that no one wants to be pecked to death.

FIND OUT MORE

Jim Tamm's talk:
"Cultivating Collaboration: Don't Be So Defensive!"
2015

Also try Julia Dhar's talk:
"How to Disagree Productively and Find Common Ground"
2018

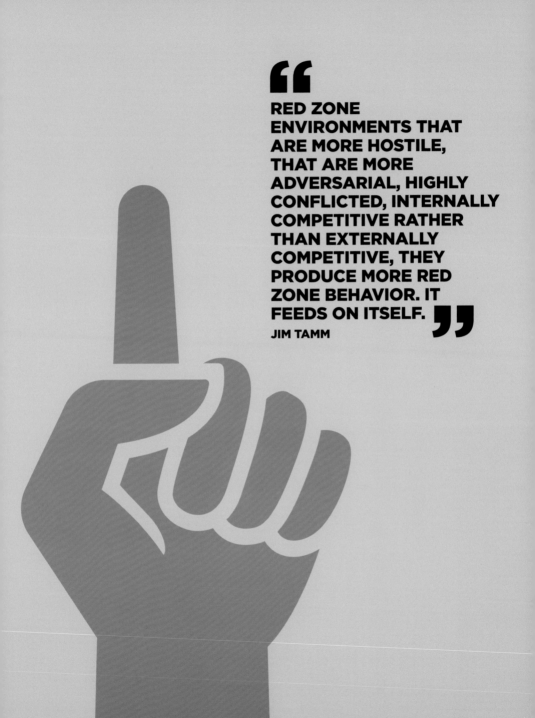

RED ZONE ENVIRONMENTS THAT ARE MORE HOSTILE, THAT ARE MORE ADVERSARIAL, HIGHLY CONFLICTED, INTERNALLY COMPETITIVE RATHER THAN EXTERNALLY COMPETITIVE, THEY PRODUCE MORE RED ZONE BEHAVIOR. IT FEEDS ON ITSELF.

JIM TAMM

BE AUTHENTIC
and don't let anyone try to change you

We all have preconceived ideas of what it means to be a leader, and often those ideas see us shy away from leadership because we fear we don't fit the mold. This chapter discusses why the greatest leaders are always authentic and explains how we can all muster the confidence to show up as our true selves.

REJECT LABELS

We like things to fit into categories, but when we allow labels to define us we can unintentionally hold ourselves back.

As one of the most successful models in the world, it seems strange to suggest that Ashley Graham would ever have felt uncomfortable telling people what she did for a living. But when she first started modeling, Graham would find herself wincing every time someone asked her. She knew that when she replied, "I'm a model," she'd quickly have to add the caveat "plus-size" because her body doesn't fit the stereotype of what some people expect from a model.

Graham starts her talk looking at herself in the mirror and telling herself

that she is bold, brilliant, and beautiful. She defines who she is for herself every day, before anyone else has the chance to do so. For most of her career she was told that because she was a plus-size model she would never book a cover shoot or walk the runway—but as she points out, she has broken through all of those expectations. Had Graham allowed the traditional definition of "plus-size model" to define her, she might never have made it any further than the odd advert. Instead, she created her own definition.

For Graham, being an authentic leader in her field meant really identifying what

> **MY BODY, LIKE MY CONFIDENCE, HAS BEEN PICKED APART, MANIPULATED, AND CONTROLLED BY OTHERS WHO DIDN'T NECESSARILY UNDERSTAND IT. I HAD TO LEARN TO RECLAIM MY BODY AS MY OWN.**
>
> **ASHLEY GRAHAM**

her purpose was—to redefine female beauty and to give a voice to young women. By defining a model in her own terms, she pulled apart the traditional label that the industry had given her and with it made something much more powerful and influential. Arguably, had she stuck with the industry's label, she would never have been as successful as she has.

It's very easy in our careers to become defined by our job title—the label that someone else has given us. But leaders know that their purpose is more important than what they're called and that it can't be constrained by a label.

Q FIND OUT MORE

Ashley Graham's talk:
"Plus-size? More Like My Size"
2015

. . . .

Also try Chimamanda Ngozi Adichie's talk:
"The Danger of a Single Story"
2009

UNCOVER

Even when we believe our workplace values inclusion, we still tend to cover up who we really are.

↗ Have you ever been told that you're "too much"? Or that you should "tone down" your personality? That was Dan Clay's experience of the workplace. When an advisor told him that he didn't need to "beat [people] over the head" with his homosexuality, Clay made it his mission to make sure no one at work would ever see his loud, flamboyant side. And for ten years his career progressed at a steady, sensible pace while he maintained a steady, sensible facade.

Then in 2016 he posted a picture of himself on Instagram dressed in drag as the *Sex and the City* character Carrie Bradshaw. It was so popular that he kept doing it, and soon "Carrie Dragshaw" had a cult following—although Clay still kept it from his work colleagues. One day, his boss sent him a message celebrating the fact that Carrie Dragshaw was in an article in *Cosmopolitan* magazine. That support gave Clay the confidence to be more open with his team, and in turn, he noticed his team became more open with him.

By uncovering who he was at home as well as in the workplace, Clay not only pushed his colleagues' boundaries around what "inclusion" actually means, but also his own. True leaders don't just set the standard of authenticity for others; they challenge their own standards, and push themselves to reveal all the facets of their personality—even those they might fear would be "too much."

🔍 FIND OUT MORE

Dan Clay's talk:
"Why You Should Bring Your Whole Self to Work"
2018

I'D PUT ON
BASICALLY
OFFICE DRAG
TO FIT
THE ROLE.
DAN CLAY

BE YOUR OWN MASTERPIECE

When we show up as a work of art, we allow other people to experience us in all our magnificence.

What would your life be like if you lived it as an artwork? That's what Daniel Lismore does. Each day he imagines that his body is a canvas, and everything he puts on that canvas is designed to create a masterpiece.

Lismore's elaborate creations are made of everything from beer cans to diamonds. He uses these materials to create a piece of art and then lives as that art. "When I get dressed I'm guided by color, texture, and shape. I rarely have a theme. I find beautiful objects from all over the world, and I curate them into 3-D tapestries over a base layer that covers my whole body shape."

For Lismore, living as a piece of art isn't just a visual experience; it allows him to experience the world around him in a different way each day. Some people love what he does and others hate it. Living this way has seen him go from private jets to homeless, but to live differently would be inauthentic to him—he truly is an artwork and that's how he wants to live. What strikes you most about Lismore is that he can never be invisible—he can't hide, and that is incredible bravery. He chooses to stand out no matter what—to be, as he puts it, "unapologetically yourself." When we do this as leaders, we allow those around us to do the same. In this way, we can start to see them as the artwork they truly are.

Q FIND OUT MORE

Daniel Lismore's talk:
"My Life As a Work of Art"
2019

> **I HAVE LIVED AS ART MY ENTIRE ADULT LIFE. LIVING AS ART IS HOW I BECAME MYSELF.**
> **DANIEL LISMORE**

STOP HIDING

The longer we hide who we really are,
the harder it is to be honest.

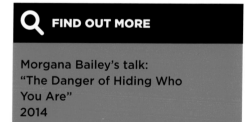

In her 2014 TED talk, Morgana Bailey finally came out, not only to her friends and family but to the world. She had spent sixteen years keeping her sexuality a secret, worried about the stigma she would face, and this secret had impacted on her behavior. While Bailey might have told herself that she wasn't "hiding" her sexuality and that she just didn't think anyone needed to know, the impact of keeping it a secret was huge. It cut her off from her friends and her coworkers, and meant she couldn't stand up when she saw injustices being perpetrated.

When Bailey moved to a company with a strong culture around inclusion and diversity, she told herself she would finally come out—but even then she didn't. Instead, she continued to hide who she was because by now it had become second nature—it was easier to continue to keep the secret than to be brave and show up as the person she really was.

It's important as leaders that we're honest with ourselves when we're keeping a secret and to ask ourselves whether we're hiding something simply because the thought of revealing it is too scary. It's part of our role to model the sort of behavior we want to encourage in our teams. So take a look at the parts of yourself you keep hidden and ask yourself if perhaps, just perhaps, it would be braver to admit who you really are.

🔍 FIND OUT MORE

Morgana Bailey's talk:
"The Danger of Hiding Who You Are"
2014

YOU'RE ALREADY A LEADER

The small actions you take every day affect those around you in ways you can't imagine.

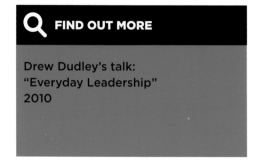

"We've made leadership about changing the world, and there is no world. There's only six billion understandings of it." In this heartfelt and funny talk, Drew Dudley tells his audience about the moment he unwittingly changed a stranger's life. He was just going about his daily life, handing out lollipops to raise awareness of a charity he worked with, and yet one lollipop resulted in a new life and a wedding. If you want to know how, you'll have to watch the talk.

But what Dudley teaches us in his talk is that how we see our place in the world might not be how other people see it. Leadership is not something we necessarily have to stand up and claim—it might be something we inhabit every day without realizing it. If other people see you as a leader, then you already are one. You don't have to take on certain characteristics or achieve a certain level of status to become a leader, you just have to accept that some people see you in this role.

When Dudley changed a woman's life, he hadn't set out to do so—he was simply handing out a few lollipops. However, she told him years later about the impact he'd had, Dudley realized how much greater his role in her life had been than he'd ever realized. So when you're thinking about who you are as a leader, ask others for their experiences of you and the impact you've had on their life. Their responses might surprise you.

🔍 FIND OUT MORE

Drew Dudley's talk:
"Everyday Leadership"
2010

GET NAKED

Not literally . . . but by being open and honest with your team, you will build trust, the most important part of leadership.

When Stephan Rathgeber asked his team to describe his style of leadership in one word, he wasn't expecting them to choose "naked." But the more he thought about it, the more he liked their choice. After all, for us to feel confident being naked around others we have to trust them, and for Rathgeber, creating a team where trust was at the center of their work was exactly what he'd wanted to do.

So, how do we create a feeling of such trust that we can be, metaphorically, naked with those around us? Rathgeber says it's based on three principles: caring, ability, and integrity. When he was made the leader of his team, he realized that the first thing he had to do was show his colleagues that he cared for them and that he wanted the best for all of them, not just himself. When he joined the team, Rathgeber made a point of diving into every task so that he could demonstrate how passionate he was about the business and how hard he was going to work. And finally, he owned his mistakes proudly (more on this in the next chapter) and kept his promises—this is what it means to act with integrity.

When you do all of this, you become a naked leader: you allow your team to see all of you, and with that you can start to build their trust.

 FIND OUT MORE

Stephan Rathgeber's talk:
"Naked Leadership"
2017

Also try Onora O'Neill's talk:
"What We Don't Understand About Trust"
2013

> **IN TIMES OF CERTAIN UNCERTAINTY AND CONSTANT CHANGE, TRUST IS THE GLUE THAT TIES PEOPLE TOGETHER.**
> **STEPHAN RATHGEBER**

MODELING SUCCESS

Are you asking your team to behave exactly as you would, or do you allow them to succeed authentically?

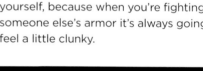

As well as studying what makes organizations function better, Courtney Bryant is also an expert in Disney films—thanks to schooling from her young nieces. They're obsessed with the movie *Frozen*, where two young princesses set out to rescue themselves. In her youth, Bryant was a big fan of the Disney movie *Mulan*, where the heroine takes up her father's armor and fights to save her people. So which movie provides a more inspiring storyline?

Letting go of her favorite, Bryant explains that *Frozen* actually represents a better model of success today because the two young leads succeed by being themselves, whereas Mulan has to take on the characteristics of her father. This is a useful analogy of why we're so concerned with authenticity at work.

Asking our team to model our behavior in order to succeed isn't definitively a bad idea—in fact, from the outside it might seem to work for them. Like Mulan, they might defeat the enemy and go on to greatness but, also like Mulan, they will have to shape themselves into someone else's armor. What *Frozen* taught Bryant, and now us, is that true success means being able to find a way through as yourself, because when you're fighting in someone else's armor it's always going to feel a little clunky.

🔍 FIND OUT MORE

Courtney Bryant's talk: "Authenticity in the Workplace" 2017

"

FROZEN **GETS THE TITLE OF THE FIRST DISNEY MOVIE WITH STRONG FEMALE PROTAGONISTS, BECAUSE ELSA AND ANNA WERE ABLE TO BE THE HEROES AS THEMSELVES, WHEREAS MULAN HAD TO LITERALLY BECOME SOMEONE ELSE. "**

COURTNEY BRYANT

VALUE AUTHENTICITY

It's one thing to say you want staff to be authentic, but how do you show them you mean it?

Only forty percent of working adults report being happy in their jobs. This isn't just bad news for them; it's also bad news for their employers. We know that workers who are happy at work are more productive and therefore generate more revenue for their organization. In his short talk "This Is What Makes Employees Happy at Work," Michael C. Bush argues that by truly appreciating their employees, businesses will not only make their staff happier but they'll make their own bottom line healthier too.

One of the simplest ways to show your staff that they are appreciated and wanted in your organization is by listening to them properly. Bush explains that listening doesn't just mean making space for them to talk; it also means hearing them with a spirit of wanting to learn and to find the best ideas possible. However, for this to happen your staff have to believe you want to hear their opinions—that as a leader you want authentic staff, not just team members who agree with you no matter what.

As Bush explains when he talks about trust, it's not enough to have this simply as one of your company's values—you have to actively show how it works. The same is true of authenticity. If you tell your staff you want them to bring their whole selves to work, rather than copying you (as Courtney Bryant explains in her talk "Authenticity in the Workplace"; see page 144), you need to ensure that when they do so they are listened to and not dismissed.

Q FIND OUT MORE

Michael C. Bush's talk:
"This Is What Makes Employees Happy at Work"
2018

CONNECTING AUTHENTICALLY

How can we connect more authentically with those around us? By using our head, heart, and core.

How real do you want to be? This is the question communication specialist and former reality TV show producer Erin Weed asks in her talk about authentic connection. The problem with asking for authenticity, Weed points out, is that very often we confuse it with transparency, leaving us feeling exposed and vulnerable.

Being authentic doesn't mean you have to show everyone all there is to you (although of course that does have value, as Dan Clay explains in his talk "Why You Should Bring Your Whole Self to Work"; see page 138). Instead, it's about using your head, heart, and core to show who you are and remaining true to your personality or character. Your head is responsible for the facts (what your name is, where you're from, and so on), your heart reveals what you feel about things and allows you to connect with others on an emotional level—feelings such as happiness, joy, and loneliness are universal, and recognizing them in others is a point of connection. And the core is what you want—your desires. Speaking from the core can feel scary, but when we do so we show others clearly what we want and we give them guidance and boundaries around how to treat us.

When we combine these three key parts, we reveal our real selves but we also have the choice of how much we reveal and to whom. And if we choose to show all three things, then we have to own it and enjoy the connection it brings.

🔍 FIND OUT MORE

Erin Weed's talk:
"Dare to Be Authentic"
2017

Also try Celeste Headlee's talk:
"Ten Ways to Have a Better Conversation"
2015

END STEREOTYPES

When we ask people to be authentic, we need to ensure we're not asking them to live up to a stereotype.

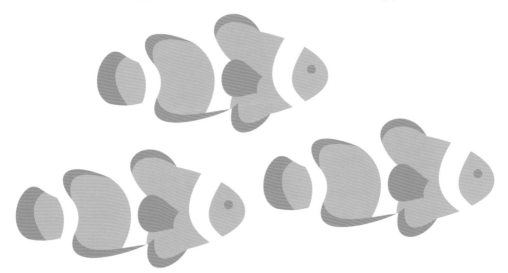

When actor America Ferrera started auditioning for roles, she noticed a strange trend. Each time she stood in front of casting directors, they would want her to be more or less Latina. It seemed everyone had a very specific idea of what Latina meant and they expected Ferrera to live up to this. It made for some awkward situations.

"When I was fifteen, I got my first professional audition. It was a commercial for cable subscriptions or bail bonds, I don't really remember. What I do remember is that the casting director asked me, 'Could you do that again, but just this time, sound more Latina.'

'Um, OK. So you want me to do it in Spanish?' I asked.

'No, no, do it in English, just sound Latina.'

'Well, I am a Latina, so isn't this what a Latina sounds like?'

There was a long and awkward silence, and then finally, 'OK, sweetie, never mind, thank you for coming in. Bye!'"

In this simple example, Ferrera illustrates the danger of expecting people to fit into stereotypes. Often when we talk about authenticity at work, we're talking about allowing people to break free of the corporate mold and bring their background and experiences into the

"

IDENTITY IS NOT MY OBSTACLE. MY IDENTITY IS MY SUPERPOWER. BECAUSE THE TRUTH IS, I AM WHAT THE WORLD LOOKS LIKE. COLLECTIVELY, WE ARE WHAT THE WORLD LOOKS LIKE. "

AMERICA FERRERA

workplace with them. But the trap we often fall into is expecting that they will show up in a specific manner depending on their age, gender, or socioeconomic background. As Ferrera points out, being Latina doesn't always match the Hollywood stereotype.

As a leader asking your team to be authentic, you need to ensure that you don't put your own stereotypes and expectations on them. Take the time to really get to know them, their views, and their values. This means listening to them and accepting them—the two components vital for an authentic workplace.

Q FIND OUT MORE

America Ferrera's talk:
"My Identity Is a Superpower—
Not an Obstacle"
2019

PICKING SIDES

Very few of us are just one thing—we have multiple roles and beliefs. Here's how to reconcile them.

When psychologist Shelley Prevost picked up Sheryl Sandberg's book *Lean In*, she was saddened to read that in nearly every culture men are seen as leaders and women are seen as nurturers. What upset Prevost wasn't simply that her gender had traditionally been seen as unsuited to leadership, but rather that she saw herself as both a leader and a nurturer, and nowhere in the world did it seem possible to be both.

As leaders, we can find ourselves feeling like we have to cut off the other parts of ourselves in order to focus solely on the part that makes us a leader. So we don't talk about our children or our partners, we forget how we act around them, and we assume that this is a different part of our personality. However, Prevost believes that it's these seeming paradoxes that make us great leaders— we don't just have to be a leader; we can be a nurturing leader. Or a funny leader. Or a thoughtful leader. We can create our own definitions.

For Prevost, authenticity finally came when she stopped trying to fit into everyone else's definition of leadership and allowed herself to define what it meant for her. Today, think about checking your own definition of leadership. Does it align with all the parts of who you are or do you need to rethink it?

🔍 FIND OUT MORE

Shelley Prevost's talk:
"Lead Like a Girl"
2015

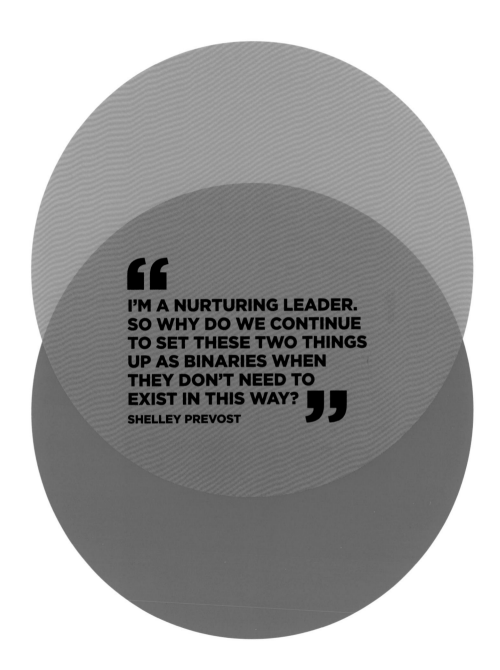

"

I'M A NURTURING LEADER.
SO WHY DO WE CONTINUE
TO SET THESE TWO THINGS
UP AS BINARIES WHEN
THEY DON'T NEED TO
EXIST IN THIS WAY? "

SHELLEY PREVOST

81/100
RISK AND REWARD

There are risks in authenticity, in showing your true self, so how do we manage those risks and still remain authentic?

The number one question professional wrestler Candice Michelle gets asked is, "Isn't wrestling fake?" But there was nothing fake in the reality of Michelle's daily training regime to become a wrestling world champion. Not least, she learned how to "bump," a style of falling whereby you land on your arms rather than your back but that still has the impact of being hit by a car traveling at 30 mph. Wrestling might be scripted, but each match has a new audience, and the reaction to that audience is real and creates a new reality for each match. Add to this the fact that each wrestler has core values, and while they might be reacting to a script they are doing it from these core values—they're bringing themselves to the show.

Above all, none of this "fake reality" happens without the hard work and dedication of the wrestlers. In order to become a world champion of wrestling you need that authentic determination—without it, you won't get anywhere. And this is the lesson of authenticity that Michelle teaches us: while the world around you might be working to a script, you can still bring your core values to that script and live as your authentic self.

In an ideal world we'd all work in places where authenticity is appreciated and required, but even when we don't we can still bring our authentic selves to the situation.

🔍 FIND OUT MORE

Candice Michelle's talk:
"The Authenticity of Fake"
2018

152 BE AUTHENTIC and don't let anyone try to change you

"

I'M SURE AT SOME POINT IN
YOUR LIFE, A PARENT, TEACHER,
PROBABLY EVEN A CLOSE
FRIEND HAS SAID TO YOU, 'YOU
DON'T HAVE WHAT IT TAKES TO
LIVE THAT DREAM, YOU'RE NOT
GOOD ENOUGH.' WELL ONLY WE
CAN PREDETERMINE OUR WIN. "

CANDICE MICHELLE

BE ACCOUNTABLE
to yourself and to everyone else

We've all seen those "the buck stops here" desk plates, but what happens when leaders really take responsibility for their actions and how does that impact their team? This chapter looks at why being responsible for your failures, as well as your successes, is so important and how to turn them into opportunities.

ACCOUNTABILITY AND FORGIVENESS

When we accept accountability for our actions, we make room for forgiveness and our own humanity.

Warning:
The following talk contains topics that some people may find distressing.

"And ever since that night I've known that there are 7,200 seconds in two hours." In one of the most powerful TED talks, Thordis Elva talks about her experience of rape. But this is not just her description of the incident, for on stage with her is her ex-boyfriend and the man who raped her, Tom Stranger. As the pair describe the incident, you can feel the tension descend on the audience and the unasked question that comes from them: "How can she bear to talk about this with him there?"

Stranger admits that it took him nine years to admit to himself what had happened and the role he had played in it.

But when Elva wrote to him, putting down her account of the experience and telling him she was still seeking a way to forgive him, so began eight years of correspondence between the two. They talked about the rape and their lives since then, and eventually they met up and spent a week talking and listening, trying to understand each other's experiences. Their determination to find a mutual understanding led them to write a book together. None of this would have been possible if Stranger hadn't been able to own up to what he had done.

We may fear admitting our mistakes, but behaving badly, hurting others, and

> ## HOW WILL WE UNDERSTAND WHAT IT IS IN HUMAN SOCIETIES THAT PRODUCES VIOLENCE IF WE REFUSE TO RECOGNIZE THE HUMANITY OF THOSE WHO COMMIT IT?
>
> **THORDIS ELVA**

hurting ourselves are all aspects of humanity, even if we wish they weren't. What we can learn as leaders from this incredible talk is that by failing to admit to the times we've wronged others, we help no one—not ourselves and certainly not them. By admitting where we have failed, we can see that this is not all that we are—Stranger calls this the paradox of ownership. By owning the fact that parts of us are imperfect, we can begin to see that we are not entirely bad, merely human.

🔍 FIND OUT MORE

Thordis Elva and Tom Stranger's talk:
"Our Story of Rape and Reconciliation"
2016

Also try Valarie Kaur's talk:
"Three Lessons of Revolutionary Love in a Time of Rage"
2017

LIES WE TELL

Deep down, we're all liars. Sometimes, however, lying is actually useful.

If I asked you if you were an honest person, what would you say? You'd probably say you were and in doing so you'd be lying. We all lie and yet we hate to admit it. But as Pamela Meyer tells us in one of the most popular TED talks of all time, sometimes we're so happy with deception that we not only lie to ourselves but we collaborate in other people's lies too.

When someone sends you an email apologizing for not getting back to you sooner because your original email "ended up in spam," you know they're lying to you. But it goes against our social contract to admit that, so we let them get away with it. It's to our benefit to accept what they're saying and so we overlook the lie—it's how every deception scheme works.

Meyer suggests that when we find ourselves collaborating in a lie, it's because we want something the lie gives us. However, we have to accept that when we do so we create a culture that values falsehood over truth. So while you don't have to call your team members out every time a "spam email" excuse comes your way, you might want to start looking at the areas where you collaborate with them to see if there's a way for everyone to be more truthful.

Q FIND OUT MORE

Pamela Meyer's talk:
"How to Spot a Liar"
2011

UNCONSCIOUS BIAS

When we base our understanding of the world solely on our own experiences, we're going to make mistakes.

"When Dorothy was a little girl, she was fascinated by her goldfish. Her father explained to her that fish swim by quickly wagging their tails to propel themselves through the water. Without hesitation, little Dorothy responded, 'Yes, Daddy, and fish swim backwards by wagging their heads.' In her mind, it was a fact as true as any other. Fish swim backwards by wagging their heads. She believed it."

Isaac Lidsky opens his talk on being responsible for how our biases shape our view of the world with this story of fish swimming backward. It is, he explains, a perfect way of summing up the strange beliefs most of us have acquired over the years and now see as truths. However, most of these beliefs are based on our experiences rather than facts, and as such we often read situations and people incorrectly.

What Lidsky is describing here is unconscious bias—the idea that our brain often conjures up a story about a person or a situation before we've had time to make a proper assessment. But he also calls for us to let this behavior go, to own up to the lies we tell ourselves and the times we've failed to look for the truth. While our behavior might be normal, it isn't good enough. We all need to try harder to look beyond our own experiences and start seeing other people's too.

To find out how your bias might be affecting your team, read Eugenia Cheng's talk on privilege (page 34).

Q FIND OUT MORE

Isaac Lidsky's talk:
"What Reality Are You Creating for Yourself?"
2016

Also try David R. Williams's talk:
"How Racism Makes Us Sick"
2016

TRANSPARENCY

If we want people to hold themselves accountable, we have to make sure they understand why their role is important.

 As a leader, you not only have to be prepared to hold yourself accountable, but also at times to hold your team accountable. When you give your team a task, you want to do so in a way that shows you trust them to get it done, and you can make that far easier for them when they understand why they are doing it.

When Tamekia MizLadi Smith was collecting data for the Office of Equity, she found it difficult to ask people personal questions about their backgrounds. Asking where someone was born or what their ethnicity was felt awkward and unnecessary. However, when she discovered how the data were used—to determine access to things such as healthcare and to monitor any inequities in this area—she realized the importance of it. Simply by understanding why she was asking the question made it easier for Smith to do a good job.

If you find your team members are not performing to expectations, ask yourself whether you've really tried to help them understand why the standards you're setting are so important? Do they understand the value their role brings? Without this understanding, it becomes impossible—and unfair—to expect them to hold themselves accountable to the same standards as someone who does understand the why. And as a leader, you're accountable to your staff. It's your job to make sure the "why" is clear, so get on and do it.

Q FIND OUT MORE

Tamekia MizLadi Smith's talk: "How to Train Employees to Have Difficult Conversations" 2018

ACKNOWLEDGE RESPONSIBILITY

When a project has failed, it can be easy to blame everyone else. Here's a simple way to establish how much was really your fault.

Stacey Abrams was the first black woman to be nominated for governor by a major political party. She didn't win, but in her self-reflective talk "3 Questions to Ask Yourself About Everything You Do," she looks at the questions she asked herself before she ran and explains how those same questions helped her plan her next move after her defeat.

For Abrams, every decision comes with three questions: What do I want? Why do I want it? And how do I get it? When we've experienced failure or things haven't gone our way, it's worth going back to these three questions and looking at your responses to them. It might be that you weren't clear enough about what you wanted to do—for example, Abrams knew she wanted change but she had to define what that change was if she was ever going to succeed at it. Or perhaps your "why" wasn't strong enough—if your heart was never really in the project, the chances of it succeeding were slim right from the start. And finally, if you weren't really clear from the outset how you were going to achieve your goal but just charged in without a plan, then you might easily be able to spot why you failed.

Using Abrams's questions to analyze our actions allows us to take responsibility for our part in their success or failure, as well as seeing where other people's responsibilities lie.

🔍 FIND OUT MORE

Stacey Abrams's talk:
"3 Questions to Ask Yourself about Everything You Do"
2018

FIGURE OUT WHAT THE 'WHY' IS FOR YOU, BECAUSE JUMPING FROM THE 'WHAT' TO THE 'DO' IS MEANINGLESS IF YOU DON'T KNOW WHY.

STACEY ABRAMS

87/100
STANDARDS OF BEHAVIOR

In order to become accountable leaders, we first have to set clear standards so that we know the behavior we are aiming for.

What is the purpose of accountability? Does it really matter whether or not we hold ourselves accountable as leaders? Cathelijne Janssen believes accountability is vital for leadership, as without it we wouldn't take the time to ask ourselves whether we are doing the right things for the right reasons and in the right way. Accountability is the thing that forces us to look at our actions and review whether we have lived up to our own standards.

One of the key traits of accountable leaders is their authenticity. Authentic leaders know what they stand for and hold themselves to their values. When Janssen was researching what made people and organizations accountable, authenticity was a defining value. In the cases where organizations or people couldn't be trusted to show their whole selves and live by their values at all times, nor could they be trusted to be accountable.

What we can learn from this as leaders is that our level of self-knowledge and a clear understanding of our own values is vital if we want to be accountable for our actions. As Morgana Bailey says in her talk "The Danger of Hiding Who You Are" (see page 141), when we hide a part of who we are it becomes much harder to hold ourselves, and others, to a standard of behavior—and therefore much harder to be truly accountable for our actions.

FIND OUT MORE

Cathelijne Janssen's talk:
"Accountability Models"
2015

"
ACCOUNTABILITY IS ABOUT TAKING RESPONSIBILITY, ACTING RESPONSIBLE, AND FEELING RESPONSIBLE ABOUT THE RESULTS.
CATHELIJNE JANSSEN "

CONFRONT FAILURE

When we fail, it's easy to feel ashamed or to believe it's because we're not good enough. It's time to reframe failure as something that's inevitable in our drive for perfection.

↗ How easy do you find it to confront your own failure? And when you do succeed, do you see it as proof that you did your very best or as a sign that perhaps the bar was too low? Recently, argues Jon Bowers, society has turned away from the idea of perfection and instead headed toward acceptance of limitations simply because we're afraid of failure. However, he believes this means we're missing out on the opportunity for greatness.

Part of being accountable for our actions and their results is acknowledging whether we really went as far as we could, and if we didn't, what held us back? When Bowers teaches delivery drivers how to be out on the road, he holds them to a standard of perfection that most of us would find intimidating. He says that whether or not they reach it is down to "a willingness to do what is difficult to achieve what is right."

As leaders, we set the standards that we want those around us to adhere to and we also have to adhere to them ourselves. When you find yourself falling short of your own standards, take time to check in with how you feel about that failure. Did it happen because you didn't put in the correct effort? Or was it simply because you were aiming high and when you do that failure is inevitable?

🔍 FIND OUT MORE

Jon Bowers's talk:
"We Should Aim for Perfection—and Stop Fearing Failure"
2017

START LISTENING

When it feels like everyone is fighting us, we can either fight back or we can take a different approach.

When the world around us keeps arguing with us, it's very easy to assume it's because we're right and they're wrong. But if we're to be truly accountable leaders then we need to be aware of the role our actions play in defining people's responses to us.

When John Francis witnessed two oil tankers colliding, creating an oil spill, he decided that he was going to give up riding in and driving cars and trucks. He started walking around his hometown, and each day people would argue with him about the validity of his protest. They felt he was walking to make them feel bad, and he disagreed. Neither side would give and the arguments continued—until one day Francis decided he would just stay silent. For 24 hours he wouldn't say a single word and he'd see what the impact was. And what happened was that he stopped arguing and started listening. And the

more he stayed silent and just listened, the more people started to understand why he'd given up cars for walking.

What we can learn from Francis's talk is the importance of becoming accountable for the reality we're creating. John was living a reality of arguments because he was taking part in those arguments, and when he stepped out of them his reality changed. What are you creating in your own life that you need to take some accountability for and how could you change it?

🔍 FIND OUT MORE

John Francis's talk:
"Walk the Earth . . . My 17-year Vow of Silence"
2009

Also try Ernesto Sirolli's talk:
"Want to Help Someone? Shut Up and Listen!"
2012

CHANGE HAPPENS

One of the reasons we fear being accountable for our actions is that we worry we can't change. But we can.

Daniel Reisel studies hardened criminals for a living. He spends his time in some of the toughest prisons talking to people who have been condemned to life sentences and branded as psychopaths. These are criminals the world thinks can't change and mustn't be allowed back into society. But Reisel believes that the ability to change is part of our humanity, no matter who we are, and as such we're all responsible for doing better in the future than we have in the past.

Reisel makes the argument that if we know through science that our brains are capable of growth and change, then we can't say, "I'm not capable of that." It might be true to say, "I'm not capable of that now," but we have the ability to move toward being the sort of person we want

to be. By holding ourselves accountable for our past actions—the ones about which we might feel shame or sadness—we admit that we're capable of changing and doing better in the future. It's this desire and willingness for growth that makes us leaders. After all, if we have no desire to grow then we'll never be able to lead others toward the future—we'll all be stuck in one place.

Q FIND OUT MORE

Daniel Reisel's talk: "The Neuroscience of Restorative Justice" 2013

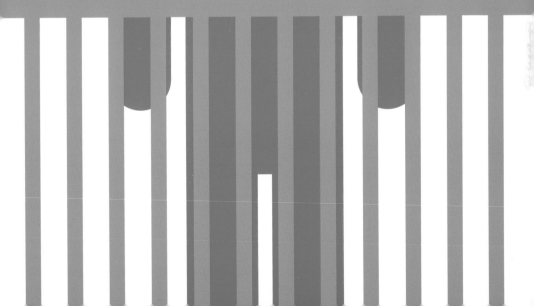

"FOR TOO LONG, I BELIEVE, WE'VE ALLOWED OURSELVES TO BE PERSUADED OF THE FALSE NOTION THAT HUMAN NATURE CANNOT CHANGE, AND AS A SOCIETY, IT'S COSTING US DEARLY. "

DANIEL REISEL

ACCOUNTABLE VISION

Quite often, problems seem too large to be tackled.
But having a clear vision helps us remain accountable.

> **HOW HAS THE SITUATION COME TO THIS, THAT WE'VE ADOPTED SUCH AN INHUMANE RESPONSE TO A HUMANITARIAN CRISIS? I DON'T BELIEVE IT'S BECAUSE PEOPLE DON'T CARE . . . I BELIEVE IT'S BECAUSE OUR POLITICIANS LACK A VISION.**
>
> **ALEXANDER BETTS**

Part of being an accountable leader is being able to admit when you've been faced with an issue that has just seemed too big and overwhelming for you to solve, and so you've pushed it to the back of your mind and gone back to your day job. In his talk "Our Refugee System is Failing. Here's How We Can Fix It," Alexander Betts forces his audience to confront a reality they might have been hiding from.

Betts talks about the refugee crisis in Europe, and in particular the public outpouring that followed the publication of photos of a small child who drowned while trying to cross into Europe. People across the globe expressed their horror and sympathy at these photos and yet, Betts tells us, in the following year another 200 children drowned because nothing in the refugee system had changed.

The toughest part of being an accountable leader can be admitting that you saw a problem and chose to do nothing about it. As was the case when people around the world who saw the refugee crisis unfolding turned away from it, there are problems that simply seem as though they are beyond our control. However, being an accountable leader means not being so afraid of failure that you do nothing, and instead having a

vision that's so powerful you can push forward to find a solution even when it seems impossible.

In his talk, Betts puts forward four solutions that might help ease the refugee crisis. He has been able to find these because his vision goes beyond managing the crisis, driving him to make a difference and to be accountable for something beyond himself. We could all use a vision that helps us do the same.

Q FIND OUT MORE

Alexander Betts's talk: "Our Refugee System Is Failing. Here's How We Can Fix It" 2016

Also try Jon Bowers's talk: "We Should Aim for Perfection—and Stop Fearing Failure" 2017

GET PRAISE

Do you feel like you've done a good job but haven't been recognized? It's time to put yourself out there and ask for praise.

Part of being a leader is accepting that if we're not getting what we need to lead well, then we need to ask for it. In her short but insightful talk on the power of the words "thank you," Laura Trice asks why, if we want praise, don't we just ask for it?

We spend most of our life being taught that to chase praise is needy or showboating, and that praise should be given sparingly in case it goes to the other person's head. In reality, getting positive feedback not only enhances our mental well-being, but it can also enhance our performance. So why are we all so reluctant to actively seek out this reassurance of our value?

Trice suggests that we're scared of asking for praise because it shows the areas where we may feel insecure or vulnerable. By asking someone to praise

us in this area, we're admitting that our own self-praise isn't quite enough. But as a leader, you need to be accountable for your own mental well-being. If there is something you need, then square your shoulders and ask for it. In the long run it will make you a better leader, and it will also help your team to thrive.

For more advice on putting yourself out there, look up Michaela DePrince's talk on standing out (page 82).

Q FIND OUT MORE

Laura Trice's talk:
"Remember to Say Thank You"
2008

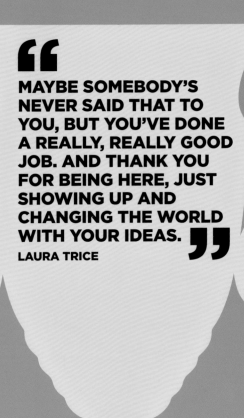

"

MAYBE SOMEBODY'S NEVER SAID THAT TO YOU, BUT YOU'VE DONE A REALLY, REALLY GOOD JOB. AND THANK YOU FOR BEING HERE, JUST SHOWING UP AND CHANGING THE WORLD WITH YOUR IDEAS. **"**

LAURA TRICE

BE AGILE— there's no time to waste on bad ideas

Technology has changed the way we work and therefore the way we lead, and businesses are now built on a "move fast and break things" approach rather than a five-year plan. This chapter explains how to lead effectively in a fast-paced environment, why teams need to be built differently, and what it means to be a leader in the digital age.

BORROW IDEAS

When you're looking for fast solutions to a problem, first look outside your own sphere of reference to see whether someone has already solved it for you.

How difficult would it be for us all to move to Mars? Well it certainly wouldn't be easy, but many of the problems that you might initially think of when you imagine setting up a colony on a new planet have already been solved, in one form or another.

In her fascinating talk on what it would take to survive on another planet, synthetic biologist Lisa Nip explains how science has already evolved in ways that make living on Mars a slightly less stressful experience than you might imagine. The key is that the science of space travel must be prepared to borrow ideas from other fields. For example, growing crops in −60-degree weather seems impossible until you realize that farmers have already started creating genetically modified crops that are designed to survive the harshest of winters.

When we, as leaders, are faced with a problem, we can sometimes feel that it is our job is to find a unique solution to it. However, when we open our eyes to other industries and technologies, we might just find that someone has already done the hard work for us, saving us time and potentially giving us a better solution than the one we would have come up with.

🔍 FIND OUT MORE

Lisa Nip's talk:
"How Humans Could Evolve to Survive in Space"
2015
. . . .
Also try Matt Ridley's talk:
"When Ideas Have Sex"
2010

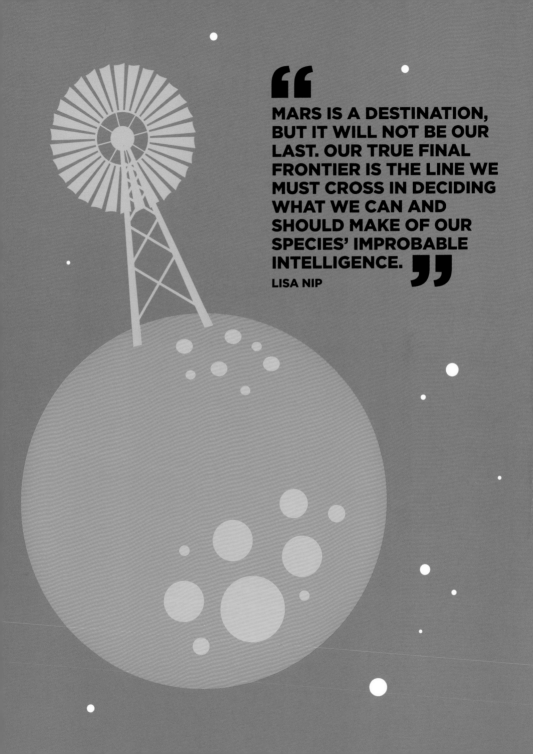

MARS IS A DESTINATION, BUT IT WILL NOT BE OUR LAST. OUR TRUE FINAL FRONTIER IS THE LINE WE MUST CROSS IN DECIDING WHAT WE CAN AND SHOULD MAKE OF OUR SPECIES' IMPROBABLE INTELLIGENCE.

LISA NIP

POWER OF PULL

Today's world moves faster and with less hierarchy than ever before. But at this speed, how do you find the things you need? You pull them in.

> **I THINK IT'S ABOUT STOPPING THIS NOTION THAT YOU NEED TO PLAN EVERYTHING, YOU NEED TO STOCK EVERYTHING, AND YOU NEED TO BE SO PREPARED, AND FOCUS ON BEING CONNECTED, ALWAYS LEARNING, FULLY AWARE, AND SUPER PRESENT.**
> **JOI ITO**

In the world that Joi Ito calls "B.I." or "Before Internet," there was a greater sense of order and structure. We knew, he suggests, that to secure funding for a business we had to create a test model, hire some MBAs to prove it would work, come up with a business plan, and then go out to get funding. But the internet changed all of that. Suddenly, anyone with a computer could create and grow a business, and funding no longer followed a specific set of rules.

With great ideas now coming from anyone, rather than solely from those who had the luxury of time and money to get an education or the contacts to push their ideas into the world, it can seem difficult to know how to create a structure that allows us to identify the best ideas and bring them to the forefront of our business. One way to manage this, says Ito, is through the power of pull—pulling in resources from your network as you need them rather than stockpiling them for a rainy day and then never using them.

What this means in practical terms is taking a look at all the connections you have, and then sorting through which ones you need now and letting the others go

until you need them. When it comes to humans this may sound harsh, but actually freeing people up to go and work on other projects allows them to put their expertise to best use and makes space for you to call in those you really need. In time, they can then be pulled elsewhere and you can pull in others, a process that allows for constant innovation and learning.

Q FIND OUT MORE

Joi Ito's talk:
"Want to Innovate? Become a 'Now-ist'"
2014

CREATE RESTRAINTS

If you want to find an innovative solution to a problem, start by limiting the resources you have to solve it.

Navi Radjou has traversed the globe studying engineers and entrepreneurs, finding the most innovative solutions in even the toughest environments. And as he's studied these creators, he's noticed something.

"In India, we call it *jugaad*. *Jugaad* is a Hindi word that means an improvised fix, a clever solution born in adversity. *Jugaad* solutions are not sophisticated or perfect, but they create more value at lower cost."

For Radjou, it turns out that the fewer resources you have, the more creative the end solution often is. As leaders, we want to give our teams as many resources as possible: we can argue for budgets and headcount, for time and space to create without the pressure of deadlines or key performance indicators. But if you want a truly innovative solution, instead try asking your team to tackle the problem when they are hemmed in by lots of others—for example, when they must create a robot without electricity or a find a new strategy in just a few minutes.

This works particularly well if you're feeling creatively burned out or incapable of coming up with new ideas. Rather than giving your brain free rein, try setting it clear parameters. You'll find that these restrictions actually help you focus and get to the answer quicker, and possibly more inventively, than you would have done when the world was your oyster.

Q FIND OUT MORE

Navi Radjou's talk:
"Creative Problem-solving in the Face of Extreme Limits"
2014

AGILE vs. TRADITIONAL

Can you bring an agile way of working to a business steeped in history and tradition? Peter Biddle thinks so.

How much agility is too much agility? This is the question Peter Biddle asked when he found himself running a start-up inside the billion-dollar company Intel. How do you go about working in an agile fashion within an organization that likes to move slowly?

For Biddle, it came down to a few key principles. The first was to decide how he wanted the future to look and then work toward making that a reality. By doing so, he not only took his own steps toward his future vision but also created a narrative so that other people could walk with him.

Biddle also deliberately kept some of these plans away from those who might have been able to help but who would have wanted to work in a way that didn't feel agile to him. He decided it was OK to say no to help that didn't fit the style of work he wanted to be doing.

> **A LITTLE BIT OF INSURRECTION IS GOOD FOR THE SOUL.**
> PETER BIDDLE

And finally, Biddle states that it's our job as leaders to make the system unfair in favor of our people. The idea here is that, as a leader, you should be going into battle for your team, finding small ways to give them space to talk about their innovations or create recognition for something they've created.

These three things lead to the final step for an agile business—"find some users and make them happy." If you do all of the above, then you'll be an agile leader in a traditional business.

FIND OUT MORE

Peter Biddle's talk:
"Plucky Rebels—Being Agile in an Un-agile Place"
2013

WHAT IF?

Teach your brain to be adaptable so that you'll be able to find an answer to whatever situation you face.

While some start-up investors might look for founders with high intelligence or emotional quotients, Natalie Fratto seeks out those with a high AQ, or adaptability quotient. She likes founders who, when faced with situations they've never encountered before, can adapt and learn from these. Such people will be able to move fast to change their strategy and make a success of something that could have been a disaster.

So how adaptable are you? Fratto suggests one simple way to test and grow your adaptability: ask yourself "what if" questions. What if there was a flood and my home disappeared overnight? What if my direct competitor suddenly came out with a new product that took over the market and left me with no customers? We can use "what if" questions to help us train our brains for the times when the unexpected does happen.

This is not an exercise to try to discover every possible problem that might arise and create solutions for these before they happen. Not only would that be impossible, it wouldn't help our brains learn to be adaptable. The goal here is not to shut down all potential issues but instead to open ourselves up to the possibility of being faced with something we haven't prepared for and being flexible enough to adapt with it. As with Navi Radjou's talk "Creative Problem-solving in the Face of Extreme Limits" (see page 180), Fratto is asking us to test how we adapt to situations when certain restraints are in place. She's giving us the opportunity to teach our brains how to flex and adapt to the information available, rather than expecting everything to adapt to us.

Q FIND OUT MORE

Natalie Fratto's talk:
"3 Ways to Measure Your Adaptability—and How to Improve It"
2019

Also try Rodney Mullen's talk:
"Pop an Ollie and Innovate!"
2012

MINDFUL CURIOSITY

One of the key things that stops us from being agile is a habit. Here's a simple way to break out of your daily habits.

While we might want to be agile leaders, it can be hard for us to break out of certain habits. When we get used to working in one particular way, shifting into another pattern of behavior can feel unwieldy and unpleasant. Even when we can see the benefits of behaving differently, we still tend to head toward our normal patterns, no matter how bad for us they might be. Anyone who's tried to give up smoking can probably relate to this.

However, Judson Brewer thinks he might have found the answer to this: mindful curiosity. During his research, Brewer found that when we use the technique of mindfulness, turning our full attention and curiosity onto our actions without judgment, we are more likely to change our behavior. His studies look at smoking and food, but the principle can equally be applied to our working lives.

As a leader, if you've had a piece of feedback that requires you to change your behavior and yet you find yourself reluctant to do so, spend some time being really curious about how you feel when you're leading in that style. What are the benefits and what are the negatives? What would be possible if you could flex your style? The more we practice this mindfulness, the more we're able to become aware of our patterns and shift them accordingly.

Q FIND OUT MORE

Judson Brewer's talk:
"A Simple Way to Break a Bad Habit"
2015

Also try Amishi Jha's talk:
"How to Tame Your Wandering Mind"
2017

AGILE AT HOME

Leadership doesn't just take place in the boardroom; we can also be leaders at home. Here's how an agile approach can help.

We tend to think of leadership as something that happens in the workplace, but the reality is that true leaders show up at work, at home, in the supermarket—wherever they're called for. And being able to bring some of your leadership skills out of the office and back to the home could be the one thing that makes your life calmer and more manageable.

It was certainly that way for Bruce Feiler. When he met a man who had used agile management techniques to bring calm to his family home, Feiler thought he might be onto something. Knowing that the principles of agile management were good communication and keeping all projects small and simple, he decided to do regular check-ins with his family.

Following the agile methodology, the meetings centered around three questions: What worked well this week? What didn't work well? And what will we agree to work on in the week ahead? These meetings transformed Feiler's family dynamic and have become some of their favorite memories.

Of course, this approach doesn't work all the time and as with any agile project, adaptability is key—if something isn't working, how can you change it? But just for a moment, try to identify some of the key moments in your family dynamic that might be better if they were managed with an agile approach? Surely it's worth a go.

Q FIND OUT MORE

Bruce Feiler's talk:
"Agile Programming—for Your Family"
2013

ALL TOGETHER NOW

To be a truly agile leader, you'll need both resilience and bravery—as well as a few other skills.

It's easy for us to say that being agile is about adaptability, but it's also about commitment. Being able to lead in an agile manner means that you'll potentially face greater instances of failure than otherwise. When we're constantly adapting and trying new approaches, the chances that something won't work out increase. Agile techniques allow us to keep these test-and-learn approaches small so that the failures are also small, but in some cases a small failure still has a big impact.

Paula Hammond's talk about the search to find a "superweapon" that could beat cancer is an example of the need for commitment and resilience, as well as an agile approach when it comes to finding a new solution. Her team has been working to create a nanoparticle that can hunt out cancerous tumors and destroy them, but as she tells her story you see how much she's had to go through to get there.

If there's one talk that brings together all the aspects of leadership that this book talks about, this is it. Through a combination of resilience, empathy, strategy, bravery, collaboration, authenticity, and accountability, Hammond has been able to keep moving forward in an agile manner. And it's this approach that allows her to celebrate how far she has come while at the same time acknowledging how far there is yet to go.

Q FIND OUT MORE

Paula Hammond's talk:
"A New Superweapon in the Fight Against Cancer"
2015

> IT'S NOT JUST ABOUT BUILDING REALLY ELEGANT SCIENCE. IT'S ABOUT CHANGING PEOPLE'S LIVES.
> **PAULA HAMMOND**

INDEX OF SPEAKERS AND THEIR TALKS

Unless another website has been stated, the TED talks below can be accessed via the TED website by typing www.ted.com/talks followed by the speaker specific link, for example www.ted.com/talks /javed_akhtar_the_gift_of_words

INDEX

ACKNOWLEDGMENTS

That this book exists is first due to the bravery of each and every one of the TED speakers. Standing on any stage can be terrifying, a TED stage particularly. So as it comes with a weight of expectations, so my many thanks to them for sharing the one idea they believe could change the world. This book also wouldn't exist without all the hard work, brilliant organizational skills and creative talent at The Bright Press. In particular, Abbie Sharman, David Price-Goodfellow, and Susi Bailey. Thank you for your patience, advice, and encouragement. And finally, many thanks to Sabrina Hirst for providing TED talk guidance and bags of enthusiasm, and the wonderful friends and family who now know far more about leadership than they ever knew they wanted to.